The Unmentionable History of the West

★ ★ ★ ★ ★

Nancy Millar

Red Deer PRESS

Published by
Red Deer Press
A Fitzhenry & Whiteside Company
1512, 1800— 4 Street S.W.
Calgary, Alberta, Canada T2S 2S5
www.reddeerpress.com

Credits
Edited for the Press by Mark Giles
Cover and text design by Naoko Masuda
Cover image courtesy Andrea Johnson
Printed and bound in Canada by Friesens for Red Deer Press

Acknowledgments
Financial support provided by the Canada Council and the Government of Canada through the
Book Publishing Industry Development Program (BPIDP).

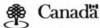 Canadä

THE CANADA COUNCIL | LE CONSEIL DES ARTS
FOR THE ARTS | DU CANADA
SINCE 1957 | DEPUIS 1957

National Library of Canada Cataloguing in Publication
Millar, Nancy
The Unmentionable History of the West / Nancy Millar.
Includes bibliographical references.
ISBN 0-88995-374-0 (pbk.)
1. Lingerie--Canada, Western--History. 2. Underwear--Canada,
Western--History. 3. Women--Canada, Western--History. I. Title.
GT2073.M44 2006 391.4209712 C2006-905451-7

Contents

★ ★ ★

Why write a book on underwear and its place in western Canadian history? Because underwear made a difference to the lives of women. It was important.

Modesty and Queen Victoria forbade almost everything in days gone by—a show of ankles, a visit to a meat market, women wearing trousers. How did women manage to meet all the standards and live their lives too?

Women's underwear through the years was all about control—corsets to die for, bras to point the way, and bloomers that drooped at the very worst moment.

Being female was like belonging to a secret society. How do babies come? Wait until your mother puts a Kotex booklet on your dresser. What about birth control? Don't mention it. Do I have to wear a bra? Yes.

Women had to get up close and personal with men's underwear as well as their own. After washing, patching, and sleeping beside their partner's longjohns, they knew very well what a trap door was and which catalogue gave the best bargains.

The female body is complex. Adding to its complications were the silences imposed upon women—silences that, years ago, kept them in the dark, in disgrace, in homes for the wayward, in the kitchen, in the soup in more ways than one.

Which came first—the women's movement or a changing trends in underwear?

"No art, no novel, no catalogue of
infamy has considered the effect of
underwear on the lives of petty rogues."
No Fixed Address by Aritha van Herk,
Red Deer Press, 1986, 1998

Introduction
We Want to Know

★ ★ ★ ★ ★

WHEN I WAS ABOUT TEN YEARS OLD, hanging around the fringes of a group of women at a community picnic, I heard one neighbor say, "All my husband has to do is put his pants on the bed and I'm pregnant." There was a ripple of knowing laughter from some of those around her and I wondered why. I had no idea what she was talking about. I noticed that my mother was not laughing. I knew then that I could not ask for an explanation. Apparently, I had stumbled onto yet another of the unmentionable subjects within our household. And for sure, I knew I could not go beyond my mother and ask the Sunday-school teacher or the schoolteacher. They would have told me to ask my mother. No one was going to help me figure it out. And once I had, I knew I could not mention it to my younger sisters. I had to join the keepers of the unmentionables. I had to be one of the silent ones.

Fifty years later, when I began the research on this book, I discovered that the mostly older women I interviewed had found their tongues and were willing to talk to me about the unmentionables of their earlier lives—the silent, personal, hidden parts. In fact, it was as if they'd been waiting for someone to ask. They shared so generously, I felt blessed.

If only I had been able to talk to the women who had come before them, their mothers, grandmothers, even Queen Victoria herself. So many rules about propriety and wardrobe came out of her era, and I'd like to know if she was as prudish

If only we knew the story of this beautiful woman in white, but the archives at the Cochrane, Alberta, Stockman's Memorial Association contain no information about her. Only her photograph survives. Has her mother told her the facts of life? Or is she going, so beautifully innocent, to face the unmentionables of female life without a clue, as so many women did? (COURTESY STOCKMANS MEMORIAL ASSOCIATION ARCHIVES, COCHRANE)

as history records her. After all, she is supposed to have told her daughter on the eve of her marriage, "Lie back and think of England." That sounds pretty matter-of-fact to me, not as starchy as she was said to be. But the fact remains that the British women who first immigrated to Canada in the 1800s as wives of businessmen or fur traders, the ruling elite of the time, came equipped with all sorts of codes and strictures about who was who, how to dress, what was decent, what could be said and what could be shown. That meant, for example, that bosoms could be shown, but the word *breasts* could not be spoken. *Limbs* could be spoken about but *legs* could not be mentioned or shown. A mere glimpse of an ankle could bring on impure thoughts.

Even the name of the river that ran through Lethbridge, Alberta, brought frowns from the matrons, who thought Belly River was not fit for polite company. The Geographic Board of Canada finally decided to name that piece of the river the Oldman since the Belly eventually ran into the Oldman.

Naturally, if women couldn't even say *belly*, they couldn't say *pregnant* or *menstruation* or *sex*, so there's very little in the written records about how pioneer women handled those unmentionable

parts of their lives. How did they manage menstruation while in a crowded colonist car coming across the prairie to Lethbridge? How did they go to the bathroom when wearing petticoats and corsets? How did they manage sex in a one-room sod shack with children in the bed across the room? How did they learn about sex, for that matter, when all mention of the act was taboo? All those things we take for granted—privacy, clean bathrooms, drugstores, doctors around the corner, more sex education than mathematics these days—did not exist for the first female explorers, pioneers and settlers in western Canada.

The private lives of aboriginal women—those who had been in Canada all along—are even less mentioned in our history books. There are hints here and there, and aboriginal women of today have helped me come up with a reasonable guess or two, but that's another subject on which formal histories are mostly silent.

As I kept trying to fill in the blanks—to speak the unmentionable—a rich and important piece of history began to emerge. The women I talked to, one of whom is 100 years old, were ready, indeed anxious, to talk about their lives, and they did so with humor, understanding, wonderment at the changes and forgiveness for the misery of some of it. They talked about how they first learned—or didn't learn—about sex, about how Kotex changed their world, about how birth control was so hush-hush, about how navy blue bloomers ruined their school years and girdles their teen years. They talked about their wedding night, their first brassiere, their last pair of nylons. They laughed at some memories, cried at others. It was real life they were talking about, and I was privileged to be there among them as they remembered. Most of them are survivors of the world before the women's movement, and they sometimes regret that their long-ago private and sometimes even public battles are not often recognized among the achievements of women. Corsets and Kotex are not the sort of things that find their way into feminist analysis or scholarly works on the history of women in the West. But maybe they should be there. After all, they shaped and controlled women in the early days as much, for instance, as restrictive matrimonial property laws did. That should surely be recognized—or if not recognized at least laughed about and shared.

There was a lot of laughter in this work. When Dawn Stephenson told me about her first bra, she laughed and called it "a horrible little harness." I laughed too because I remembered my own horrible little harness. At its introduction, it was also embarrassing, restricting and painful, but with Dawn, so many years later, I laughed. What else could we do? When it was first presented to us, we put the thing on and got on with our lives. Did it shape our lives in more ways than one? Most certainly.

Perhaps the problem is that good, modest women over the last 200 years of western Canadian history haven't communicated their stories. Many of us were brought up in an age when to be female was to be silent, with eyes cast down and ears closed to anything that might have explained our lives. We knew silence. But if my recent interviews with so many women are any indication, then we're ready to speak up, to say our piece, to mention the unmentionables and to claim recognition for the strength they represent.

So here now are tales of the unmentionable. For several reasons, I've stayed within western Canada to find these stories. First of all, we're barely out of the shell. In 2005 both Alberta and Saskatchewan celebrated their centenaries as provinces. Being only one hundred years old makes us different from

"By tribal custom, all the old women of the past are my grandmothers." —Beverly Hungry Wolf

other parts of Canada. Secondly, I live here. It's my own history. The pioneer experience is just one or two generations away from my own. My interest was also sharpened by the many local histories that have been produced in the last thirty to forty years. I love them. They are a wonderful resource, but they miss whole chunks of women's lives. Mrs. Homesteader, we are told, had twelve children, three of whom died as babies and were buried in the pasture by the barn. Tell me more, I ask. But there is no more. No more about possible birth control, about home remedies that were or were not used to keep those babies alive, no more about the despair and loneliness of having three babies buried in the pasture by the barn. No more, for that matter, about the rules that bound the lives of the girl babies who did survive, who married in their turn and had twelve babies, three of whom died. And so on.

And then there's the fact of our diversity. The West started out as home to a number of aboriginal Canadian and American tribes. But there weren't many of them per square mile, and Canada had a lot of square miles. Then, added to the mix in the eighteenth and nineteenth centuries were fur traders and explorers from the British Isles and France. Then came the missionaries, who were followed shortly by immigrants from all over the world—Russia, China, England, America, Poland, the Ukraine—who came because the prairie west had land. We offered immigrants a good deal: it was called homesteading. So they came, they saw and sometimes they conquered. My dad came from Denmark in 1923. Sometimes he conquered—and when he didn't, he spoke optimistically to us kids about "next year." We were a next-year bunch. All the settlers were or else they didn't survive.

And lastly, I've stayed with western Canadian women because I wonder deep down if we didn't become stronger because the frontier was do or die, life or death. There was no going back. As the daughter of pioneers in the Yorkton area of Saskatchewan remembered, "If there had been a bridge across the Atlantic Ocean, mama said she would gladly have walked all the way back to Sweden that first winter." But, of course, there was no bridge, no way to go back; so she stayed and bore a daughter and made a life. That's typical of women everywhere. But we in the West have been through the process of nation-building more recently, and the words and strengths of the original pioneers are still with us.

*How did this brave woman in a huge hat manage her personal life as she and her family headed north to the
Peace River country on the Edson Trail? She had to walk and ride through hundreds of miles of bush and mud.
There are no bathrooms along the way, just bush, no stores to provide supplies, no time to wash out unmention-
ables, no privacy. How did she manage? We're never told.*

I am grateful to all the women who welcomed me into their lives. I enjoyed and treasured every interview. Special thanks to one woman, Faye Reineberg Holt, who set me on the right path for this project and laughed and cried in all the right places. My thanks also to Jennifer Hamblin and Lindsay Moir at the Glenbow Museum in Calgary who let me browse through old catalogues to my heart's content and who never once murmured about my strange interest in men's and women's undergarments. In short, thank you all for your help and encouragement. I am full of good cheer because I hope I have turned the lives of ordinary women into History with a capital *H.* So many women said to me, "I didn't know I was important." Guess what. You are.

Chapter 1
We Had Our Dignity

★　　★　　★　　★　　★

I BEGAN THIS BOOK, ODDLY ENOUGH, because of a story about a man's long underwear. A Saskatchewan farmer's wife wrote to Prime Minister Bennett in 1933 asking him to send her husband a new pair of long underwear. His old pair had been patched until there was nothing left to patch, she explained, and he had to have underwear to endure the work on their homestead through the winter. What's more, if he didn't get new long johns, they'd have to leave the land and give up their dream of building the West. Thus, please see the pair on page such-and-such of Eaton's catalogue, pay for, and send it to us, she asked.

And he did. The prime minister of Canada came through with the very pair that she had ordered, all paid for. And who knows, maybe that one pair of long johns kept them going long enough to make a go of it on their farm in the West.

So at least in this instance, it can be said that underwear built the West as much as railways or immigration schemes or wheat. And since no one had written a book on the rise and fall of the trap door, I began hunting up stories about long underwear. They were certainly part of my youth in the Peace River country in the 1940s and 1950s. There was hardly a yard you could drive into without seeing several pairs of men's underwear flapping on the clothesline or drooping over the back fence. Long johns were often referred to in local history books as well, but it occurred to me one day during my research that articles of female underwear weren't often mentioned in book or song, and for sure I knew they never showed up on clothes-

Made By Wolsey

Eatonia
"GOOD VALUE AND
RELIABILITY".

The
Underwear
For Value and Comfort

lines in the old days either. Newly washed bras and panties were hung to dry inside a pillowcase or folded up inside towels in order to maintain the family reputation. So I added corsets and girdles and other horrid harnesses to my underwear research, and that's when my son suggested that I was studying the unmentionable history of the West.

The word *unmentionable* led me into other invisible areas: how women learned about sex, how they managed menstruation before the whole subject turned up in living color on television, how they managed their reproductive lives when they couldn't even say the words, how garters ruined many a date. These things are not mentioned in history books, not even in the local history books that so many communities have published in the last forty years. They are wonderful resources, but they leave out so much about the practical, personal details of women's lives.

The fact is, women just didn't talk about their private lives in earlier times, so their absence in history books is not unusual. Ninety-five-year-old Alexa Church of Balzac told me simply, "We had our dignity," and I respect her for that. But as long as the missing parts are kept quiet and private, the story of women's valor in building the West isn't

complete. If a woman managed to cross the prairies dressed in long skirts, petticoats and corsets while dealing with menstruation or perhaps pregnancy, she's stronger than we give her credit for. She deserves more than the praise she gets for skills like butter-making. There are so many references to women and butter making in local history books that I'm moved to wonder just who was left to eat the butter. But it may be that butter-making is the safest metaphor for all the work women did. Nanci Langford, an Edmonton academic and historian, explains:

These images and stories we perpetuate in hundreds of community histories represent both what we wish and what we believe our heritage to be. They also represent what we do not know, and sometimes dare not speak about, and that is the work of women that is invisible and yet essential to survival, the unacknowledged pain and silent suffering of many homestead women, the vast diversity of women's experiences and accomplishments unknown to us.

Still, she says, the local history books are very valuable records even though "they are too modest and share little of the meaning and complexity of women's lives."

If the lives of pioneer newcomers are under-reported, what about those of the aboriginal women, constantly on the move through prairie and bush? What did they do about those awkward moments in their lives? They must have had systems, rites of passage for the whole female experience. Whether nobody's asking or nobody's telling, I don't know, but their stories are very hard to find.

For that matter, what did my mother do when she taught school in remote northern Alberta? She had to board with a family near the school and sleep with one of the daughters of the family. How did she find the privacy to manage her body? Maybe that's part of the reason she didn't like teaching. I wish I'd asked her.

Of course, she would have told me to mind my own business. I can hear her now. But mom, you're wrong. How can I understand my own life unless I can relate it to what's come before? How can my daughters make sense of the world they're in if they can't pin it to a foundation? Bad pun there, for I do talk about foundations eventually—corsets, girdles, and other harnesses, the whole lot of them a black hole in women's history. But I'm going to begin with the rules that women lived under. Not rules about paying taxes and driving on the right side of the road, but rules about modesty and decorum, how to sit and how to behave, whom to speak to and whom to snub, who's on first and what's on second. Mostly unwritten, these rules had to be obeyed or a woman would find herself outside the circle looking in.

We can point the finger now at Queen Victoria, she who set the standard for the Victorian era, where a flash of stocking was simply shocking, as the song goes. But Victoria was a product of her time. As we all are. One day even the smartest, most modern woman of the 2000s will be looked at critically for some behavior or attitude and be regarded simply as "a product of her time."

Queen Victoria and Mrs. Grundy

Queen Victoria gets a lot of the blame for the strict rules of modesty that governed the behavior of Canadian men and women in the Victorian era. And so she should. She was the titular ruler of a very big chunk of the world, and her standards, both literally and figuratively, held the day. But even though she was

Opposite: This is the same kind of suit of long johns that the farmer's wife in Saskatchewan asked the prime minister to order, pay for and send to them— which he did, and maybe saved the West by doing so. (EATON'S CATALOGUE, FALL AND WINTER, 1934–35)

the monarch, she still had to follow rules. Take the matter of her marriage. When Prince Albert of Saxe-Coburg-Gotha came to the castle to be inspected as possible husband material, Victoria was immediately smitten. "It was with some emotion that I beheld Albert—who is beautiful," she wrote in her diary. Of course, she couldn't say those words. She had to work through the etiquette of court, the rules of engagement and protocol. She couldn't even dance with him at one of the parties held at the court in his honor. To dance together would have required him to put his hand about her waist, and that would never do. So she looked at him longingly, and he pressed her hand tenderly. That sealed the match.

The next day, she summoned him—yes, summoned him—and invited him to marry her. "I told him," she wrote later, "that it would make me too happy if he would consent to what I wished." Smart man, he consented. They were married on February 10, 1840, with all the pomp and ceremony attendant upon such an occasion. When they retired to their private rooms, she wrote in her diary that Albert "called me names of tenderness. I have never yet heard used to me before—was bliss beyond belief. Oh, this was the happiest day of my life! May God help me to do my duty as I ought and be worthy of such blessing."

She writes again the next morning and becomes almost personal about her wedding night, as close as any proper Victorian woman could get perhaps. "When day dawned (for we did not sleep much) and I beheld that beautiful angelic face by my side, it was more than I can express. He does look so beautiful in his shirt only, with his beautiful throat seen."

You can't help liking Victoria as a young woman in love, experiencing compliments and lovemaking for the first time. She never gives specific details even in her diary, but she does say they sat together for a while before she had to leave to be "laced." That would be the end of any cuddling since to be laced meant to be tied tightly into one's corset. From then on, her body would be unavailable, encased in whalebone and laces and shrouded in petticoats and dresses with skirts so wide she couldn't walk through an ordinary door. The little queen and her Albert could only enjoy their bodies once the laces were undone.

More or less nine months later, the queen's diary reveals that a baby girl was born. "Oh, Madam," the doctor said, "it is a girl."

"Never mind," said the queen, "the next will be a prince." Cabinet ministers and church officials were in a room next to the delivery suite, there to verify that the child actually came from the queen's body. Remember that next time you get angry at Queen Victoria. Did you have to have parliament in the room while you gave birth?

A few days after the birth, she asked her doctor if Albert might read to her. No, the doctor said, a novel would be far too exciting in her condition. Better to lie around in complete boredom for a while longer. So she asked if Albert might read from the Bible, and that was allowed.

As predicted, the baby prince appeared the next year, followed over the years by seven more children. Not that the queen would have asked for advice on birth control, since that was one of the most unmentionable of all subjects, but had she broached the subject, she would have been given the wrong advice. Doctors then thought that intercourse was safe in the middle of the woman's cycle, which we know now to be the very best time for conceiving. The only alternative was abstinence. However, by all accounts, Victoria and Albert remained a devoted and loving pair, although the queen did say in a letter to her daughter years later:

All marriage is such a lottery—the happiness is always an exchange—though it may be a very happy one—still the poor woman is bodily and morally the husband's slave. That always sticks in my throat. When I think of a merry, happy, free young girl—and look at the ailing, aching state a young wife generally is doomed to—which you can't deny is the penalty of marriage.

This is liberated talk for a queen who is portrayed as one who wouldn't say "sex" if her life were full of it. Maybe that was the point. It was saying the words that was the problem. Mrs. Grundy would certainly have agreed.

Mrs. Grundy was a minor character in a minor play in England in 1798. She wasn't a real person at all, yet Mrs. Grundy came to stand for all the petty rules about morality and dress in England in the 1800s. A female character in the play constantly asks, "What would Mrs. Grundy say? What would Mrs. Grundy do?" These questions became such catchphrases that people began to believe there really was such a woman who was constantly censoring them. If a woman wore the newfangled colored underwear, Mrs. Grundy's dis-

When I asked in an interview why pregnant women had to hide their pregnancy under maternity tent dresses and smocks, Alexa Church said simply, "It was the modest thing to do. We didn't discuss such things. It was private."

ciples shuddered and declared it wouldn't do. Mrs. Grundy said so. *Colic, bowel,* and *stomach* could not be spoken in decent company. *Breasts* had to be *bosom.* *Legs* became *limbs,* and as for the pregnant woman, she might just as well have gone to the moon because there were no permissible words with which to describe her situation. Mrs. Grundy apparently didn't approve of the words *breeding* or *with child* or *lying in,* and what she would have done with the bold word *pregnant* is impossible to imagine. Pregnant women went into *confinement* and didn't come out until the baby was born.

Men couldn't escape Mrs. Grundy either. Their underwear could only be referred to as *linen.* Trousers were *inexpressibles* or *nether integuments.* And that which happens between men and women was just not discussed unless it occurred with big words in poetry when it became *passional relations* or the *union of souls.* Even doctors had to beat around the bush about intercourse when speaking to their patients. Dr. J.B. Keswick, in his book about conjugal relations counsels:

> If ever a husband urges on his wife a relation that will subject her to the liability of maternity when she does not wish it, he must govern his passion. His soul will thus shine with deeper luster on his manhood.

With such rules of propriety in Queen Victoria's time, it's no wonder that to go into the sea for a quick dip she had to be encased in many layers of clothes and stay inside a canvas that moved into the sea with her to hide her bare feet—the only uncovered part of her.

You may think all this had nothing to do with Canada in days gone by. On the contrary, the public image of "Victoria the Good" and prim and proper England very much dictated attitudes and behavior in the colonies at that time. In Manitoba, for example, Michael Ewanchuk, a child of Ukrainian immigrants, remembered that his first reader had a picture of Queen Victoria on the first page and that the school flew the Union Jack. What did he know of either? "But we had to be in the school before the Union Jack was hoisted or else we were late." And if they were late, they'd have to make their peace with the queen or at least her representative, the teacher, with the strap.

When in Doubt, Consult the Rules

Queen Victoria died in 1901, but her standards lived on. These were the post-

The Sears Roebuck catalogue from 1901–02 bristles with "unmentionables," but you have to read between the lines. There are lightly boned corsets known also as waists and there are wire bustles and feather-filled bustles to create fullness in the hips. If it's fullness in the bust you need, there's the wire-form item Number 87. And finally, there's even an early form of menstrual pads and a belt to hold them - items 90 and 88.

ed rules for a teacher in Alberta in 1905:

- You will not marry during term of your contract.
- You must be home between the hours of 8:00 P.M. and 6:00 A.M. unless attending a school function.
- You are not to keep company with men.
- You may not loiter downtown.
- You may not smoke cigarettes, cigars, or pipe, or chew tobacco or take snuff.
- You may not, under any circumstances, dye your hair.
- Your dress must not be any shorter than two inches above the ankle.

Even thirty years later, teachers were still under careful community scrutiny. Alexa Church was teaching in Didsbury when a young female bank clerk, new to town, asked her to go for coffee one evening. As they sat in the local restaurant, the bank clerk lit a cigarette. The next day, the secretary of the school board took Alexa aside and told her it was not appropriate for a schoolteacher to be seen with a woman who smoked. It just wouldn't do. Alexa obeyed. She - could have lost her job if she hadn't.

In another central Alberta area, a widowed farmwoman engaged a hired man to help her keep the farm going. Community standards being what they were, she couldn't be alone with a single man in her employ and certainly not in her house. So she married him—only to have him leave her high and dry, taking her team of horses and walking plow with him.

A widow who wanted to keep the farm found a man to marry; a man who lost his wife married another woman to have help with the children. These were practical arrangements. There was no other way. A grown man and a grown woman could simply not live together under the same roof unless they were husband and wife. These second marriages often worked out well, but there was no guarantee.

There were so many rules. When a farmwoman died in rural Alberta, her neighbors rallied to help the family. One neighbor realized that the six-year-old daughter of the deceased woman had nothing good enough to wear to the funeral, so she made her a new dress. The father refused to let his daughter wear it. He felt it was indecent because it didn't touch the top of her shoes. So the child wore her old dress.

Edith Cavell would have understood his standards. She was a British nurse working in a British hospital in Brussels when the German army occupied the city in 1915. When a suspicious number of Allied soldiers escaped to the Dutch border, the Germans accused Cavell of aiding and abetting the escapees. She admitted her guilt and was sentenced to death by firing squad. As she stood in front of the guns, did she beg for mercy, protest her fate? No, she carefully pinned her skirts together at the hem so that her "limbs" would not be revealed after she was shot and fell to the ground. Propriety mattered, even in the face of a firing squad.

Propriety mattered even in the mountains, or so Mary Schaffer Warren discovered. When she first came to Banff, Alberta, in 1889 from her home in Pennsylvania, she was a proper lady. The daughter of wealthy parents, wife to a doctor, she was the kind of woman who knows her place. As Janice Sanford Beck records in her biography, Schaffer Warren fell in love with the Rocky Mountains and discovered that mountains didn't care whether she was a proper lady or not. As she explored them, she didn't always wear her hat "to protect her delicate complexion," she didn't always ride sidesaddle and, worst of all, she occasionally wore pants.

The local paper huffed and puffed that "Pants are made for men and not for women. Women are made for men and not for pants." That remark was printed in 1908, the same year that Mary Schaffer Warren "rediscovered" Maligne Lake, all the while wearing her breeches. Maybe if she had called them a "divided skirt" the newspaper's editorial writers might have felt more comfortable.

Just a glimpse of ankle was enough to get a woman into trouble. Faith Fenton, a reporter for the *Toronto Globe*, was sent to the Yukon to write a story on the gold rush in 1898. When her boat stopped en route at Wrangell, Alaska, she walked down the gangplank for a look at the town and was observed by local women to be showing a bit more ankle than was decent. Lt. Colonel T.B.D. Evans was promptly informed of the problem. He was the officer in charge of a contingent of the Yukon Field Force being sent north to support the RCMP in maintaining Canada's sovereignty in the region. Strong men and true they may have been, but Evans feared they would be driven mad with passion at seeing Fenton's ankles. So a married woman on board was asked to have a quiet word with the sinner. By the time the boat left Wrangell, Fenton's dress sported a

No problem with pants for these children of pioneers in the ranching area near Calgary. They are Hope and Harry Hargrave, and they haven't yet heard of Queen Victoria and her rules. (COURTESY STOCKMANS MEMORIAL ASSOCIATION ARCHIVES, COCHRANE)

border of black sateen around the hem, blocking any view of ankles.

Roosters, of all things, caused some flutters when British women came to live in western Canada. Back in England, they called male birds "cocks," but when they did so in Canada, brows were raised. Dorothea Allison, British born and raised, described such an incident in a letter to a friend back home:

Here, in Canada, they never talk of 'cocks and hens.' It is most indecent here to mention a cock even on a Ranch. You must call cocks Roosters. Isn't it funny? At first I must often have made the other Ranchers' wives blush—I naturally spoke of killing off my cocks for the table—but I have found it most indecent to mention a cock.

While Canadian women were blushing at Mrs. Allison's talk of cocks, she was having trouble with some of their terms as well. "A nice little Canadian woman came to call on me the other day and over a cup of tea told me she had a 'gassy stomach' and 'female trouble,'" she recorded. Another good lady wanted to 'leave the room' so I showed her to the bathroom where I keep a P.O. She

said it wouldn't do as she wished to 'relieve her bowels.' I promptly dispatched her to the outside club of course." The outside club would have been the outhouse, the P.O. a portable, inside commode. These beat-about-the-bush words were the Canadian way of being proper.

Maggie Gilkes' mother grew up in South Africa, the product of British parents who did not allow their innocent daughter to go into a meat market. It wasn't proper in those days for young girls to see raw meat. Then she married an equally proper British man, and they decided to come to western Canada, where they would become farmers. "My parents were right out of their element," Maggie remembered years later. "They were classically educated people who believed the British way was the right way. Canada didn't turn out as they had expected." They farmed and did the best they could, but there were so many compromises. Their daughters not only saw raw meat, they helped cut it up. The girls had to ride a horse to the school miles away, so they wore pants, the same kind the boys wore. And even though the pants were absolutely necessary and eminently sensible, it still hurt to see their "limbs" so exposed. Eaton's catalogue, the most popular book in western Canada but not exactly the classic literature of their upbringing, graced their outhouse, serving a purpose other than reading just as it did for every other hardscrabble farm. It was a long way from Queen Victoria.

Still, the Victorian standards of behavior and dress were the underpinning of their lives, so they and others like them passed on to the next generation all the rules and standards of their homeland. The rules were watered down by circumstances and distance, but they were there, which is why, in the 1920s, newly married Grace Budgeon was not able to wear her new red dress to a community card party. Her husband protested that she looked as if she was "asking for it." Red couldn't be worn by young women. That too was a leftover from other times, other places.

There were so many rules with so many shadings that women must have longed for a simple list: Do this, don't do that; say rooster, not cock; don't let your bare arms show. That's why local women's organizations like the Women's Institute, the Ladies Aid and the United Farm Women became so important in the development of the West. The members didn't so much list the expected rules of behavior and beliefs as they simply lived them. The newcomers watched and learned.

Stay on Your Own Side of the Boulder

Queen Victoria didn't manage the modesty of the world all by herself. She had lots of help from the Christian churches. Judy Schultz, in her book *Mamie's Children*, tells of one such incident:

There was this one man, Brother So-and-So. I forget his name. He was a raving evangelist, a real hellfire and damnation type. He set up this big tent and we all went to the meeting. I remember one thing in particular. My mother wore a georgette blouse to church. Real pretty, you know, with long sleeves, but that material was kind of flimsy and you could see her arms through it. Well now, he preached about it all through the service, condemning her for immodesty, going on about Eve tempting Adam and I don't know what all else.

The preacher may even have called her an "impertinent hussy." That term was reserved for any woman who

In days gone by, biffies were expected to be hidden from view—in a patch of trees or behind the barn perhaps. However, the wide open prairies made it difficult to hide the inevitable outhouse so some people just put it out front and blamed it on Maw. (AUTHOR'S COLLECTION)

stepped over some perceived line of modesty—like the woman at English Bay in Vancouver in the late 1800s who dared to step beyond the boulder. In those days, men and women couldn't bathe together at that popular ocean beach. Women had to be on the west side of a big boulder, men on the east, and never could the sexes meet. It would be immodest for women to be seen in their bathing costumes, although the costumes—more like a dress with a flounce around the middle—pretty well covered up any sign of the female body. You had to use your imagination to see beyond the layers. According to one writer, the flounce looked much like a mud guard hanging off the back of a car.

If you didn't obey and stay on your side of the boulder, Joe Fortes would move in. He was the unofficial lifeguard who kept the men from wandering over the line. It was normally the men who got too close. But one day a woman decided to move into male territory. Joe had never had to deal with a woman before. What's more, this one wasn't wearing stockings and sandals as proper women did. She was actually naked from her knees to her feet. Joe was stymied. And the woman boldly walked where no woman had walked before.

A lively tempest in a teapot ensued. City council met to discuss options, newspapers covered the affair in great detail in editorials that asked what the world was coming to. Finally, the Women's Christian Temperance Union weighed in. This was a dedicated group of churchwomen who usually battled against the sale of liquor. Here, however, the uproar was over the perceived immorality of a woman walking around in her bathing costume. They wrote a stern letter to a local paper condemning the actions of the "impertinent hussy." And they must have used some other strong words as well because the impertinent hussy sued the WCTU for damages—and won. It's still known as the Great English Bay Scandal.

But by the early 1900s on the prairies, rules about modesty had to be adjusted to local conditions. Take the case of Harold, a young student minister who was sent to an area of Saskatchewan to make a list of all the settlers and their church affiliations to see if any marriage ceremonies or baptisms were required. Harold set out on horseback. Fighting his way through a sudden snowstorm, he saw the light of a small log cabin in the distance. There he found a farmer, his wife, a buxom daughter, a younger daughter and a young man. They welcomed him with open arms, fed him a good meal and listened with delight to news from the outside world. Eventually, the younger daughter disappeared through the one door that opened off the living area. Then the older daughter said her goodnights, followed shortly by the mother and father. "I'll just make myself comfortable in the barn," Harold said. The young lad protested, "Oh, no need. Mam has made arrangements for you if you don't mind sleeping alongside me."

So they blew out the candle and went through the one door to where, as far as our visitor could see, there was one bed. His companion peeled down to his underwear and got into the bed next to the wall, or so it seemed. Being a proper Englishman, the young churchman undressed completely, put on his pajamas and crawled in. As he was dropping off to sleep, the bed moved, but his companion had not. What was happening? That's when he put up his hand to touch the wall and realized it was a sheet hung from ceiling to bed. The rest of the family was on the other side of that sheet.

As a proper Englishman, he was shocked by this turn of events, but there had to be safety in numbers, so he slept. The next morning, however, he had to fake sleep while the mother and father got up first, then the daughters, then the boy next to him. Only then did poor Harold leap out of bed and put his clothes on over his pajamas. It was a quick lesson in the adjustments that have to be made in frontier days.

It took some nuns, surely the most modest and proper of all women, to demonstrate the art of making adjustments without losing modesty. In 1844 a group of Grey Nuns from Montreal decided to establish a mission in the Red River area of Manitoba. They hired a group of French Canadian voyageurs to take them to their destination. The men were willing, strong and always polite, but as they paddled, their songs were sometimes rather too blue for the ears of their passengers. The head voyageur constantly hushed his men, but the songs helped them keep rhythm as they paddled. They were used to them. They needed them. It was up to the nuns to protect their virtue. So they devised a plan. Either they'd read the Bible loudly or pray throughout the singing, or they'd try to change the naughty words to nicer ones. The third option worked best. The nuns just quietly began to sing along with the men, but they sang different words, a cleaner version. The men quickly picked up the new words and used them. Modesty was maintained.

What About Those Who Had Been Here All Along?

Aboriginal women had lived in the land now known as Canada for thousands of years. It was their home. When white men came to this new land, bringing with them white women and silly rules about cocks and roosters, these women suddenly found that they too were in a new land with new rules. They adjusted to the new ways for the first 100 years of exploration and fur trading in the West. Some married fur traders, country fashion, and raised a capable breed of mixed-race children. Some simply grew to appreciate the goods that the traders had for sale: iron pots and kettles, knives, awls and cloth. Others stayed away from the newcomers and carried on as they had for centuries.

It was white women who upset the balance. With the coming of white women, the unique and important characteristics of the aboriginal women, and the skills they brought to daily living, were devalued.

The explorers and fur traders were conditioned to see beauty and accomplishment through European eyes. When they first arrived in Canada, it was all very well to take an aboriginal woman as a companion, have children with her and use her skills in any way possible. But she could never be as "womanly" as a British woman. She was uncultivated, not "proper." To be fair, a number of the men who took country wives were loyal to them to the end. David Thompson was one. When he left off mapping and exploring and moved to Montreal, he took Charlotte Small with him. They are buried side by side in the Mount Royal Cemetery, although David gets many more words on their grave marker than Charlotte. Still, he stayed with her to the end. He did not "turn her off," a term used when a fur trader returned to England or Montreal and more or less passed his country wife on to another trader.

But once European women began joining their husbands in Canada, the relationship that had developed between British and European men and aboriginal Canadians changed drastically. Aboriginal women were suddenly seen as lacking—lacking propriety (they didn't know a breast was a bosom) and lacking proper gentility (they had their children with less fuss than white women). And they didn't know the first thing about Christianity. Preachers, who had also arrived in Canada by that time, made a great deal of trouble over who believed what, and a great deal of trouble too about marriage and why every man should marry one of his own kind. Forgotten were the strength and loyalty and hard work that the country wives provided. Forgotten also were the children.

The children. There's the rub. It was one thing to "turn off" your country wife and expect her to go back to her people, but it was quite another to say good-bye to the children whom you had grown to love. Many fur-trader fathers tried to do right by their children. Sons could be set up in the fur trade, but daughters needed husbands, and that meant they needed an education and proper clothing. But even that wasn't always enough. As Sylvia Van Kirk concludes in her book *Many Tender Ties:*

The introduction of white women into Rupert's Land was to have profound implications for fur trade society: It gave the men a choice of marital partners that could prove detrimental to the position of mixed-blood women, even if they had become quite 'English' in their manner.

Suddenly, the daughters of white couples trumped the mixed-race girls who just a few years earlier were sought after, even if those all-white daughters couldn't make a moccasin or endure a Canadian winter. Suddenly, there was a return to snobbery about class and color.

The first written documents about the aboriginal women of Canada appear in accounts of the Red River settlement, established in the early 1800s. Until then, aboriginal women seem to have been almost invisible, a handy resource but not worth mentioning in any detail. There's the odd word here and there in the diaries of some of the earlier fur traders. Peter Fidler, for example, seems to have been a nice man who faithfully recorded the date and place of birth of each of the fourteen children his wife, Mary, bore him. On August 18, 1821, he officially married Mary, so she might have legal standing in his affairs after his death.

But even as Peter Fidler was doing the right thing by his Mary, the church was of two minds about such liaisons. The minister who wed them recorded the occasion simply: "Peter Fidler of Manitobah & Mary, an Indian woman of the same place, were married at Norway House, this fourteenth day of August 1821 by me. (Signed) John West, Chaplain." Mary is simply Mary. She's given no last name, and there's no attempt to identify her as anything more than "Indian."

The tensions between white and aboriginal came to a head in the Red River settlement with a huge scandal in the mid-1800s. Sarah Ballenden was a mixed-race woman, good looking, the wife of the area Hudson's Bay Company manager, at the top of the social heap. She loved her life as chatelaine and was good at it. Her parties sparkled, she sparkled, her baby was named Frances after the wife of George Simpson, governor of the Hudson's Bay Company. The world was her oyster—until, that is, some British-born wives decided she was getting a little too big for her britches. After all, she was mixed-race, and it did seem as though one of their own kind, Captain Christopher Foss, was just paying her a little too much attention.

Finally, Foss fought back against the gossip with a suit of defamatory conspiracy to "clear the reputation of a Lady," he said. He won the suit but lost the war. After the gossip and the excitement of the trial, Sarah's reputation was ruined forever. White women were the only ones who could be truly moral and upstanding. Aboriginal or mixed-race women just didn't have it in them. Poor Sarah was guilty because of her race. Sadly, she died a few years later, a "fallen woman."

Woman Doctors? Run for Your Lives

Women were always doctors, even when they weren't allowed to be doctors. Aboriginal women knew about herbal remedies; they delivered one another's babies; they looked after wounds, broken bones and disease. So did European women for that matter—it was a female sphere. But when medicine became a profession, a set curriculum of studies, it was taken over by men. Not that women weren't still in the front lines of medical care for the family. They just couldn't be trained or regarded as doctors.

Once again, the problem was modesty. How could women possibly take medical training when they'd have to learn anatomy, which meant they'd have to look at a male body? Compounding the problem, how could male students be expected to concentrate when women were in their midst? It was unthinkable. So it couldn't be done. Women were not allowed into medical schools.

Emily Stowe was the first Canadian woman to officially challenge the rule. The Toronto School of Medicine refused to admit her. So she studied in the United States at the New York

Medical College for Women, graduating in 1867, the same year that Canada became a nation. Still, Canada wasn't big enough or strong enough to license a woman doctor. So Emily Stowe operated a clinic in Toronto without a license. Her patients, mostly women, didn't care. They were so glad to have a woman care for them. During the 1870s, Emily and another brave woman, Jennie Trout, attended a session at the Toronto School of Medicine, where they were subjected to a barrage of crude jokes and drawings from their instructors and fellow students, all male. But they persevered, and both got their license to practice medicine in Ontario.

Dr. Stowe didn't stop there. With amazing energy and determination, she became a crusader for women's rights to higher education, to the vote and to equal rights under the law. No wonder her daughter, Augusta Stowe Gullin, became the first woman to obtain a medical degree in Canada and the first female professor of medicine.

Not that the problems were solved. When Jennie Smillie Robertson graduated in 1909 from the University of Toronto medical faculty, she couldn't get operating privileges at any of the city hospitals. Possibly the powers that be at those hospitals realized she had

not been allowed to take certain anatomy courses with the rest of the male class and had had to study parts of the subject through pictures. No matter. She joined other female doctors and founded Women's College Hospital in Toronto, where she was Chief of Gynecology from 1912–42.

Dr. Amelia Yeomans and her daughter, Dr. Lillian Yeomans, both took their training at the University of Michigan and arrived in Winnipeg in 1885, just in time for the North-West Rebellion. Manitoba may have been too busy with other things just then to notice, but somehow the two women got their medical licenses and were officially the first female doctors in the West. Both specialized in midwifery and the diseases of women and children. But Amelia didn't stop there. All around her she saw poverty, awful housing, unemployment, inadequate sewage facilities, inadequate public support. She even spoke out about prostitutes, saying they were not fallen women but women who had no alternatives. Added to all that, she began campaigning for the vote for women. "Women are the most adamant protectors of community morals, purity and righteousness and will use their votes accordingly," she argued. She won that battle posthumously. In 1916 Manitoba granted women the vote—the first province to do so. Although Yeomans had died three years earlier, her causes had not.

Years later, women were still being treated differently than men in medical schools, as Marlene Mackie relates in *Gender Relations in Canada*. In the 1940s Phyllis Steele and one other woman in the Faculty of Medicine at the University of Alberta were not allowed to attend classes on the subject of male genitalia because it was feared it would be too embarrassing for them. Still, they were expected to take an oral exam on the subject. Phyllis read her textbooks and turned up for the exam. The presiding professor from the Department of Urinary Diseases asked one question only: "How much cinnamon do you put in an apple pie?"

He was obviously already offended at her effrontery in presenting herself for the exam. Not wanting to offend him further, Phyllis swallowed hard and said, "A teaspoonful, sir."

He shut his exam book with a snap and said, "That's all a woman needs to know. You can get out now."

Chapter 2
We Had Our Supports

★　　★　　★　　★　　★

WOMEN'S UNDERWEAR HAS BEEN THROUGH SO MANY UPS AND DOWNS, ins and outs, highs and lows—sometimes all at the same time—that it's hard to keep track of continually changing styles and rules of fashion. As Oscar Wilde put it, "Fashion is a form of ugliness so unbearable that we are compelled to alter it every six months." Or, today, maybe every three months. Change comes faster than it used to.

Fashion—with a capital *F*—has always been perceived as primarily a woman's affair. It has been studied, if at all, through the disciplines of art history or costume art, but is now moving into social history, cultural studies and even philosophy. So the next time you're accused of thinking too much about clothes, you could say you're studying philosophy.

Consider the long-forgotten slip, a descendant of the petticoat. It was the garment that, until the 1960s, a woman wore immediately under her dress to conceal all the underpinnings beneath. A slip was also a sign of decency. If you sported a slip, a bold sunbeam shining through your skirt would never reveal your legs. Remember the shock in 1980 when a photographer caught Princess Diana in a dress with the sun behind her? We could clearly see the silhouette of her legs. It was a big deal. Although in calendar time the event really wasn't that long ago, in underwear time it was eons ago. Who would care now if Diana's legs were shown? Who even knows what a slip is anymore? I never see any evidence of a slip today unless

Until the 1960s, every women was sure to wear a slip under her dress. This jazzy advertisement from a 1957 Chatelaine *suggests the slip as part of the foundation for fun and elegance.*

I'm in a seniors' residence, where I sometimes see a slip strap peeping out or an edge of slip showing.

This brings back such memories. In my younger days in the 1950s, to have any part of the slip showing was a major faux pas. At a glimpse of an errant strap, some older woman would advance and whisper, "Your strap's showing," at which point I knew I had to get out of the public eye and do something about it. With any luck, I'd have a safety pin with me so that I could find a quiet corner and pin the escaping strap to my dress—or my skin, if necessary. A slip drooping below the hem of one's dress was much harder to fix, but it too was a matter of great concern. Again, we girls had to find a quiet corner, a bathroom or, if all else failed, an outdoor biffy, and haul our slip up by the straps and hope it would stay there. If it didn't, there'd be talk the next day.

The talk would be personal and private—one mother to another, the Canadian Girls in Training leader to the girl with slip issues. Now it's the subject of academic discourse. In the article "Dress and Embodied Subjectivity" in *Body Dressing*, Elizabeth Wilson analyzed the reactions to slip problems as "something more than slight sartorial sloppiness but the exposure of some-

thing much more profoundly ambiguous and disturbing . . . the naked body underneath the clothes."

The naked body. The bottom line in years past. Do not cross that line. Until, that is, you get to the twenty-first century when it's quite all right be as naked as one likes, to wear as little or as much as one likes. How did that happen when the fashion world exists to keep turning out clothes that we are supposed to want to buy and wear? The answer is that fashion never stands still. Right now we're in a show-everything stage. Wait a while and we'll be covered up again.

In fact, fashion is an ever-changing drama with its own language. The older woman with a slip strap peeping out at her neckline speaks one language, the young woman with low-rise jeans and a belly stud speaks another. Age is revealed, of course, but so is social standing, money, political leanings, tribal connections, class. And sometimes fashion in dress is all about getting undressed, our clothing sometimes saying, "I'm willing to be unclothed."

Where does the body fit into this elaborate scheme of clothing and fashion? Is the body merely an accessory to the look, or is the look an accessory to the body? If I wear a suit to an afternoon meeting, am I a different person from the one who goes to an evening soirée wearing taffeta and lace? I'd have to answer "sort of" to that question. So does that say that I am what I wear?

I think not. For if I were to look at a dress in a museum, one from Victorian times, say, I'd notice the dress and all its features, but I'd also be thinking of the body that must have worn it, how slim she must have been, how hard it must have been to drag all that fabric around. So I'm imagining that dress on a body. I'm embodying it. Body and dress as a package. Sometimes more of the body is in the equation, sometimes more of the dress.

That's where fashion comes in. It's always reinventing the body, concealing some parts, revealing others. The Victorian woman would never have let her "limbs" show beneath her skirt, but she displayed a good deal of bosom. Flapper girls of the 1920s bound their breasts, but freed their legs in order to have the "It" look. The "New Look" came along in the 1950s and required yet another kind of body presentation, another set of underwear.

Corsets and Girdles: The Ugly Stepsisters

The big question about corsets is why did women wear them? Why wear some-

These women have to be wearing corsets—not that either Alice or Ada Sculthorpe would have needed them. But a woman was not properly dressed unless she was properly corseted. Alice, right, was a dressmaker who moved from England to Maple Creek, Saskatchewan, in 1905 and then to the Peace River country of Alberta. When the family home caught fire, Alice rescued two things: her coat and the sewing machine.(COURTESY GLENN AND AUDREY GRUBB, WEMBLEY, AB)

Mary Small married Seymour Bomford in Medicine Hat in December 1892. Her wasp waist would have met all the Victorian standards of the day. (Courtesy Esplanade Archives, Medicine hat, Alberta)

thing that cut off breathing, made childbirth dangerous and rendered physical activity impossible? Why wear a garment that makes going to the bathroom an awkward struggle? Is following fashion really that important?

Well, yes, it is, especially when it is combined with status as it was in Europe from whence came Canadian standards. Beatrice Fontanel, author of *Support and Seduction: The History of Corsets and Bras,* insists that European women never challenged the rule of the corset in the 1800s because it signaled superiority:

Those wearing it were barred from even the slightest useful exertion, thus reinforcing the prestige of the ruling class. Women of the aristocracy felt that to wear a corset was more vital than health itself, so imperative was the need to distinguish oneself from the common people.

Ivan Sayers of Vancouver, museum consultant and clothing historian, explains the attraction of corsets as "beauty by impairment." The more a woman was impaired by her clothing and appearance in earlier times, the greater was her influence. In fact, it was her duty to be uncomfortable, if neces-

sary, because on her shoulders rode the entire social position of the family.

For years, the chief measure of accomplishment was simply the smallness of a woman's waist, though achieving such smallness came at great cost. The properly corseted woman could only take sips of water or tea for fear she might have to go to the bathroom. That's why Victorian women in novels are always swooning—they're dehydrated. Activity was pretty well limited to walking sedately down country lanes, embroidering, and reading. When British women first came to the Red River area, they expected to have servants who would do the hard work, but even with that, they learned to lighten the layers and loosen the stays. Otherwise, they couldn't manage a household. They couldn't continue to let their clothing impede their lives.

Meanwhile, the servant doing the work in the back kitchen had her own version of a corset, but it didn't count. It was a bodice that laced up the front and was worn over the dress. It might have been pretty, she might have been pretty, but her corset laced up the front—and that established her lack of status. A woman with status had servants to help her into her corset, which laced up the back—an important distinction. The kitchen maid, however, could at least breathe.

No woman of the upper class would have mentioned corsets in polite society, of course, but they were there, always lying in wait underneath everything else. They were the most visible invisible part of Victorian life. Never just an undergarment, but a way of life.

Some British private schools for girls advertised a course known as Waist Control. Don't worry about anything for the mind. They would take your darling daughter and reduce her waist to a specified measurement. You want sixteen inches? Done. They'd keep her on a diet and—most important of all—they'd gradually tighten her corset strings until, through the course of the school year, sixteen inches was achieved. *H* for Hourglass. *D* for Deadly.

When Isaac Singer patented his sewing machine in 1851, it became possible to accommodate a woman's body shape with gussets and panels of strong fabric, instead of torturing it into shape with whalebone and steel. This also meant that corsets could be tighter, so doctors began warning pregnant women to leave off their corsets during pregnancy. Pregnant women then had to go into "confinement" since they couldn't be seen without the proper underpinnings.

Bustles became popular in the 1860s, which meant women might not have needed to lace their corsets so tightly. With a bustle added to hips and rear, the waist looked smaller without actually having to be smaller. Bustles did add bulk, however, and that was good. Layers, weight and bulk indicated wealth and prestige. They meant you had to have servants to look after you, and that included helping you through doorways and in and out of carriages. "Beauty by impairment" became "prestige by impairment."

Then in the 1880s, Dr. Gustave Jaeger began his campaign in England to have everyone wear wool next to the skin to "prevent the retention of noxious exhalations of the body." Suddenly, health was in, and Queen Victoria sponsored an International Health Exhibition in London in 1884. But that didn't mean corsets were out. The big news was "rustless" steel, which meant that corsets would last longer—a dubious achievement perhaps. By the end of the century, steel workers had figured out how to bend narrow threads of steel into spiral shapes that could bend in all directions. A hurrah for corset-makers, another shallow breath for women.

However, no matter how the corset changed through the years, it maintained its role as arbiter of who was in

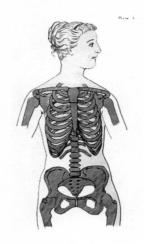

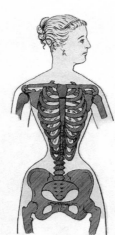

These sketches illustrate the malformation of the body caused by corsets. (Courtesy Andrea Johnson)

and who was out. It spoke a language of its own—that the wearer was worthy, that this was the right way to behave and look, and if you didn't behave and look that way, then you were less worthy and so you lost. Proof of that attitude lay in the fact that one of the first things aboriginal and Métis girls had to do when they were sent to residential school was to change their underwear. From the mid-1800s through to the 1930s in western Canada, they were issued what was called a "waist," a version of the corset known as a corselet. It came complete with garters to hold up their stockings, and over it they had to wear bloomer underpants. The girls couldn't be decent unless dressed in this manner.

And so the corset continued to rule all through the 1800s and well into the 1900s. The Eaton's catalogue of 1889 offered "Corsets by thousands, literally thousands," and added as part of the sales pitch that:

In selling so many corsets, we get to know their adaptations. A couple of lines for instance make themselves more prominent than others, not because they are right for everybody, but because we sell them by hundreds and guarantee them, with the makers to back us.

How to guarantee a corset when customer and seller are hundreds of miles apart is hard to figure, but those first catalogue companies managed somehow and provided a great service for their remote and isolated customers.

Also, how did those first catalogues manage to mention corsets and other unmentionables to a public not used to unmentionables being mentioned? In the end, the catalogue writers met the challenge by settling on no-nonsense descriptions. Just the facts, ma'am. A description from the 1889 Eaton's catalogue contains words only, no pictures:

The genuine Coraline (a derivative of the cactus plant) is superior to whalebone and gives honest value and perfect satisfaction, and Dr. Ball's health preserving Corsets, the side sections of which are made elastic by the use of fine coiled wire Springs, are warranted to outwear the corset. The money paid for them will be refunded after three weeks trial if not perfectly satisfactory in every respect. Of course, the makers think they are perfect, and so they are, if you want what the makers think you want.

Courtesy Wikipedia

The list of specific corsets includes the following:

- Drab corsets, seventeen cents per pair.
- Corset with double steel front, thirty-five cents.
- Crompton's Coraline Corset, $1.00 and $1.25 per pair.
- Ball's Circle Hip with coiled sides, $1.00 per pair.
- Thompson's Glove Fitting X Brand, English make, $1.40 per pair.
- Crompton's Abdominal Corset, elastic gores and lacing in sides, $2.00 a pair.
- Lily, steam molded, long waisted and perfect fitting, $1.75, extra sizes 30–36, $2.25

There was no problem with modesty and rules since the description was words only. The trouble began when line drawings of underwear appeared. The corsets in particular were a bit too curvy for some people's taste. Letters were dispatched from women's church groups to Timothy Eaton himself. More letters followed when women's bodies were drawn inside the corsets, bras and girdles. Just one more attack on propriety, the protesters cried. But

all of that paled in comparison to the outcry when real women were photographed wearing real underwear. It was disgusting and shouldn't be allowed, the critics said. Too much skin showing, too much temptation for men, a loss of dignity for women.

However, two world wars changed many things, including women's underwear. The corset began to lose some of its strength, both literally and figuratively, and in its wake came the girdle, a piece of underwear that was, at various times in its history, as awful as any Victorian corset. But women bought into it. Even slim women wore girdles. Why? To hold up the stockings, true, since the dreaded garters were hung on the dreaded girdles. But there was more to it. Women wore girdles because it was the right thing to do. It indicated class, status.

Status again. A 1940s advertisement for a Gossard girdle told women to be "Glorified by Gossard." That's all it would take to be glorious—a new girdle. It was the same theory behind corsets a century earlier. Wear a corset, you're somebody. You're worthy. Wear a Gossard and you're glorified.

Of course all that glory was supposed to remain underground, as it were. What would Queen Victoria think of the recent trend of wearing

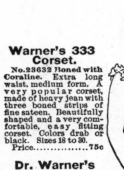

Warner's 333 Corset.
No. 23632 Boned with Coraline. Extra long waist, medium form. A very popular corset, made of heavy jean with three boned strips of fine sateen. Beautifully shaped and a very comfortable, easy fitting corset. Colors drab or black. Sizes 18 to 30.
Price................75c

Dr. Warner's Health Corset.

In spite of the modesty of the times, corset companies didn't hesitate to use advertising to sell their products. The descriptions in the 1897 Sears Roebuck catalogue stress "fit" and "service."

underwear as outerwear? Madonna in her bustier would have given her apoplexy, bra straps as fashion statements would have meant a stern lecture. You can be sure that many a conversation is taking place in homes today about these newest trends in women's clothing. But maybe that's another lesson to be learned from corsets and girdles: that a change in underwear can hurt in more ways than one.

What Frances Wore in the Bush

In 1830, Frances Simpson became the bride of her cousin, George Simpson, governor—also known as emperor—of the Hudson's Bay Company in Canada. Frances had no idea what she was getting into. She was eighteen, a sheltered daughter who had grown up in London in proper circumstances with proper connections. George, on the other hand, was forty-three years old and had been in Canada for many years, constantly traveling throughout the West to Hudson's Bay Company posts by canoe to supervise the operations of the far-flung fur trading empire. On his travels, he enjoyed, indeed expected, the company of aboriginal women, and any children that resulted from these liaisons he dismissed as "bits of brown."

Alberta historian Grant MacEwan remarked that George Simpson must have had at least seventy children scattered throughout the Northwest, but Frances likely heard nothing of that, since proper women were supposed to be too delicate to hear such tales. Aboriginal women were apparently able to hear them and bear them.

George eventually decided he should marry a proper lady, went courting and settled on Frances. They were married in London, England, and sailed to Montreal. Then George had the bright idea that Frances should come with him on a tour of the major fur trading posts across Canada. He might even have said it would be fun. They'd go by canoe, the voyageurs doing all the work. All she had to do was enjoy the scenery.

Frances, bless her, went along with the idea. But think of it. How did she manage to cram a voluminous dress circa 1830 into a canoe? How did she drag a long skirt and petticoats through portages and muskegs and bush? How did she manage to stay ladylike and cool while mosquitoes nibbled her bare bosom? For that matter, how did she go to the bathroom? She couldn't exactly ask the voyageurs to stop at a handy clump of bush. It wouldn't do to be so personal. As one Victorian lady was quoted as saying, "These are not

Frances Simpson made her first trip to western Canada dressed in all the complicated layers of clothing appropriate for a proper British woman in 1830. There are no photographs of her in a canoe, but another Frances—Frances Hopkins—painted this picture of herself in 1869 in a canoe on a Canadian river. It gives us some idea of the practical problems that European women must have encountered while traveling in this manner. (COURTESY THE NATIONAL ARCHIVES OF CANADA)

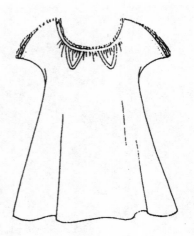

A woman of means in the 1830s would have put on a chemise first, then stockings held up with ribbon or some sort of suspender. Then would come the corset, laced in the back and heavily boned to make the waist as small as possible. On top of this would go the open-crotch drawers and several petticoats. Last of all came the full-skirted dress, a shawl and a hat.

things, my dear, that we speak of; indeed we try not even to think of them." What about her periods? Now, there was a truly unmentionable subject. Just what did this eighteen-year-old innocent do in the Canadian wilderness with a new husband who wasn't exactly innocent himself?

Obviously, she coped because she got back safely back to Montreal and a few years later back to the safety of London, where George visited her every now and then.

But let's look at what Frances must have been wearing on that canoe trip. There was a maidservant or two along, of course, because Frances would not have been able to manage her corset by herself.

First, she would have been helped into a chemise, a straight knee-length garment of cotton or linen worn next to the skin under everything else, to protect the next layers from perspiration. Then on would go the stockings, to be held up by a ribbon tied beneath the knee. (A few years later, Charles Goodyear invented an early form of elastic, but it wasn't available yet to hold up Frances's stockings.) Then would come knee-length knickers (or drawers) with an open crotch, looking like two pant legs joined at the waist and fastened with buttons or ties. They sound a bit drafty, but

it is thought that open crotch knickers or pantaloons allowed women to urinate standing up. Such an explanation leaves unanswered questions as to the particulars of these maneuvers. Frances would still have needed help to pull her petticoats and dress away from the action.

After the drawers came the corset, the all-important construction to turn a woman into a lady. Even in a canoe, Frances would have worn her corset. She wasn't a lady without it, and George had chosen her because she was a lady. So the corset stayed. Unfortunately, it would have been one of the older models that had to be entirely removed in order to change the tightness of the stays. Therefore, she would not have been able to adjust the tightness as the day in the canoe wore on. A few years later, a new system of busks and eyelets was devised so that that a corset's strings could be loosened through a system of loops and hooks. The busk was the wooden or whalebone rod that kept the front of the corset flat. With the new system, a woman could loosen her stays without undressing entirely. Thus came the term "the loosening of the stays." However, Frances would not have had the pleasure of loosening. Once she was laced into the construction in the morning, she would have been held captive for the day. Also new in the 1830s were metallic eyelets that strengthened the fabric around the laces so that the laces could be pulled even tighter without tearing out. A dubious benefit, one might guess, for Frances in her travels.

There was no bra as such in 1830. The corset ended just below the breast, but there was a camisole, the one piece of underclothing that was allowed to peek out through the layers, especially if it was bordered with French lace or embroidery. Also allowed to peek through the layers was the bosom. You couldn't show legs (or "limbs"), but you could display a generous amount of front—an interesting contradiction.

Then came the petticoats, which in the 1830s were fairly manageable. (By the mid-1850s, they were out of control entirely, one of the rules being that every lady should wear at least twenty pounds of petticoats plus the crinoline hoops that became fashionable then.) In 1830, however, Frances would not have been loaded down with more than several pounds of petticoats.

Lastly, her hat would have weighed at least five pounds, and she would have been expected to wear it at all times. Probably it kept the sun out of her eyes and protected the delicate complexion that every real lady was supposed to have, but it must have been tricky balancing it going through rapids on the Red River.

From birth to death, Frances Simpson lived in corsets. They defined her time and her place. The only time she might have been able to maintain her place in society without them would have been in the Canadian wilderness, in a canoe, visiting fur traders and aboriginals who knew nothing of the messages that corsets sent. But Frances *was* her corset, her corset was Frances. She couldn't have taken it off.

A War Changes What Women Wear

It was 1916 in Manitoba. Queen Victoria had been dead since 1901. With her went the most extreme rules about modesty. However, the rules about dress lived on through the Edwardian age (1890–1916) when corsets were constructed to make a woman's body form the *S* shape, the absolutely latest thing in fashion. The bosom was pushed forward and the bottom pushed backward so that when a woman's figure was seen in silhouette, it formed the all important *S*. Naturally, this shape required the generous help of a long lean corset to form the *S* and to make the waist as small as possible. In some cases, the corset had to be so long that it impeded a woman's ability to walk. She hobbled. So around 1910,

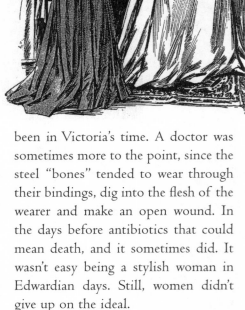

fashion came up with the hobble skirt. Beauty by impairment again.

Steel, rather than whalebone, was used in corsets by this time—bad news for women. Whalebone had at least warmed to a woman's body and allowed a bit of give if necessary. Not steel. Once you were laced, you were bound for the day. But women could now adjust the laces themselves if things got too tight because laces had moved to the front of the corset. A servant wasn't as necessary as it had been in Victoria's time. A doctor was sometimes more to the point, since the steel "bones" tended to wear through their bindings, dig into the flesh of the wearer and make an open wound. In the days before antibiotics that could mean death, and it sometimes did. It wasn't easy being a stylish woman in Edwardian days. Still, women didn't give up on the ideal.

Even World War I didn't cure women of the corset habit. Oh, they took it off to milk the cows or bring in the hay while their men were away fighting overseas, but most put it right back on as soon as they could. They were respectable women, after all, and respectable women wore corsets, didn't they? But then the men came home, the lucky ones, and for some reason or other, the women started taking off their underwear. Maybe it was the euphoria of the end of war. Maybe it was money and a booming economy. Maybe it was the effect of movies and magazines that brought the lifestyles of the rich and famous to everyone who could read or see, but whatever caused it, it was a lovely interlude in the 1920s known as the Flapper era. Women took off their corsets, donned little slinky short dresses, rolled their stockings below their knees and danced their nights away. At least, that's the popular image of those years. In truth, most women in Canada's West didn't have the money or opportunity to dance the nights away, but they loosened up. Some still wore a corset, but it would have been longer and leaner in order to go beneath the flapper styles. Girdles arrived, lighter and without bones, and the word *brassiere* began to appear in catalogues. Slips were worn instead of petticoats, a source of some comfort to mothers who figured the slip was at

least another layer before "heaven's gate," a term that meant *vagina* but was also used to mean seduction.

Some young women went so far as to bob their hair—something that was a big adjustment for their mothers. Thelma Levy, a young schoolteacher in the 1920s, couldn't resist getting her beautiful long hair cut into the new short bobbed style. She felt so daring, so young, but when she went home for a weekend to visit her folks, her mother took one look at the short hair and "her face just went white. She thought I must be a fallen woman," Thelma recalled many years later.

You can see why mothers were concerned. Their daughters could now actually feel their dresses move against their skin as they danced their way through the decade. That had never been possible before when there had always been layers of clothing between skin and dress. Was the world coming to an end?

In a way, it was. The economic recession, called the Depression in western Canada, came along after the stock market crash in 1929 and spoiled everyone's fun.

Girdles: Back with a Vengeance

Corset-makers fought them, older women scorned them, but girdles began

Irene Parlby was photographed in her proper Edwardian presentation gown in England before she emigrated to Canada. Once here, she turned her attention to the needs of rural women in the West. She was the first woman to become a cabinet minister in the Alberta government and was one of the Famous Five who fought and won the battle that gained Canadian women recognition as persons under the BNA Act. (COURTESY GLENBOW ARCHIVES, NA 2204-11)

Near right: Grace and Vera Rosaine of Drumheller wore their "divided skirts" in public in 1919. It was still an unusual choice for women, but the fact they were called knickers or jodhpurs may have made them more acceptable. (AUTHOR 's COLLECTION)

Far right: Women who had to do farm chores while the men were away at work or war may have borrowed the men's overalls to get the chores done, but they quickly changed back to women's clothing when the work was finished. (COURTESY RED DEER AND DISTRICT ARCHIVES)

Someone had to do the harvesting while the men were overseas during World War I, so two farm wives from the Souris area of Manitoba climbed on their mowers and began the job. But not without their long skirts and sunbonnets. (COURTESY ARCHIVES OF MANITOBA, B669)

to get a hold on the underwear industry in the 1920s, and that hold got stronger every year. Literally. A girdle was a wide belt that supported the body from waist to thighs. Some styles were mean to the body, others kinder. Those worn under flapper dresses were fairly forgiving: a few bones perhaps and some sturdy stitching, but a woman could still breathe. However, with improvements in elastic and the introduction of latex and two-way stretch fabrics, girdles gained a lot of control. Not for the faint hearted was a roll-on girdle of the 1950s. This was a piece of rubber that looked quite innocent in its rolled up state, but when unrolled and pulled up one's body it became a tyrant. Anything that squeezed the belly area had to push the extra flesh out some-where, which left women with a spare tire above the girdle. That in turn had to be brought under control by a long-line bra, reinforced with a few steel inserts. The combination was as uncomfortable and restricting as any-thing Queen Victoria would have approved.

The war years, 1939–45, let women breathe for a while because both steel and rubber were rationed. Ivan Sayers' mother was in the Canadian Women's Army Corps (CWAC) through the war years and used to delight in reciting this war ditty to her son and friends:

Ships of steel for even keel
Need tons and tons of corset steel.
Army trucks if they're to hurdle
Need the rubber of the girdle.
The time has come the gods have written
Women now must bulge for Britain.

It made a good joke. But women really weren't supposed to bulge. Then as now, there was a sense that slim was best, that women who "let themselves go" weren't as worthy as their slimmer sisters. The least they could do was wear a girdle and keep it under control. Such snobbery extended to young teens as well, which is why the word "corselet" entered the underwear world. It was an undergarment meant to prepare young girls for their future by holding their organs in place, forcing good posture and maintaining the modesty necessary to guarantee a good future—that is, to get a man. In her essay, "Growing up Female," Veronica Strong-Boag notes, "No more than their mothers could girls easily mould themselves to fit the figure of the day or escape the message that any other body shape ultimately brought into question both their femi-

This illustration was published in 1928, one year before the stock market crash and the ensuing economic depression. The fashions are still flapper in feeling: long, lean and somewhat revealing. Underwear was minimal. Mothers worried.
(Courtesy Chatelaine magazine)

Even in the Dirty Thirties in western Canada, when women had to make their old corsets stretch in more ways than one, advertisements still urged the corseted look. (COURTESY CHATELAINE MAGAZINE)

ninity and their ability to compete for boyfriends and husbands." The corselet was eventually sold to older women, as well as a lighter foundation to be worn during sports or housework.

Through the 1940s and 1950s, every decent woman wore a girdle or a short corset under her house dress and especially under her Sunday-go-to-meeting dress. Before the 1960s, when the underwear revolution began, underwear was a matter of respectability, not a matter of choice. It didn't matter if you were slim and didn't need girdling. You still needed the dreaded garters to hold up your stockings, which were also required for respectability. There were some who made do with rubber jar rings to hold up their stockings and left their corsets in the closet, but it was a matter of status. Wear your underwear or lose status.

Certainly, the woman who made famous the words, "You can never be too rich or too thin," wore underwear in spite of her thin, rich body. Wallis Simpson, an American divorcée, married the Duke of Windsor in 1937 and became the wife of the man who wouldn't be king. She and the Duke traveled the world visiting exotic places like High River, Alberta, where the Duke had a ranch. On a visit in 1941, the Duchess came to a branding look-

ing very proper, not a hair out of place, wearing a black skirt and jacket with a coat thrown carelessly over her shoulders. Underneath, no doubt, she wore an expensive French girdle, said to be the best in the world, silk stockings held firmly in place by the garters attached to the girdle, a bra of the very latest design, lace-trimmed panties— the kind that would have to be hung on the clothesline inside a pillowcase to prevent "impure thoughts"—and a slip. Slips were a must in 1941, and the Duchess's was probably finer and lacier than most.

The Duchess would have had no problem buying her underwear. Couturiers likely came to her mansions with samples and took her orders personally. But in the wilds of western Canada, where could women get their personal clothing? In rural areas, the country stores didn't carry much in the underwear line. Besides, there was the issue of privacy. There were always people around, men discussing crops or elections or Johnny's two-headed calf. And even in the larger centers, did you really want the storekeeper's daughter to know your measurements and the state of your thighs? One solution was the traveling salesman, also known in parts of Alberta as the Syrian peddler. In coal

Lingerie was a favorite gift for wives and sweet-
hearts during the World War II. Here soldiers from
Canadian Forces Base Penhold, Alberta, line up in
Osborne Ladies Wear in Red Deer, Alberta, to buy
a little something for the little woman. (COURTESY
RED DEER AND DISTRICT ARCHIVES)

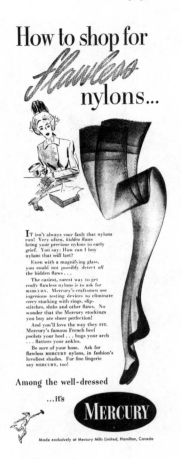

How to shop for *flawless* nylons...

IT isn't always *your* fault that nylons run! Very often, *hidden flaws* bring your precious nylons to early grief. You say: How can I buy nylons that *will* last?

Even with a magnifying glass, you could not possibly detect *all* the hidden flaws . . .

The easiest, surest way to get *really* flawless nylons is to ask for MERCURY. Mercury's craftsmen use ingenious testing devices to eliminate every stocking with rings, slip-stitches, slubs and other flaws. No wonder that the Mercury stockings you buy are sheer perfection!

And you'll love the way they FIT. Mercury's famous French heel *pockets* your heel . . . *hugs* your arch . . . flatters your ankles.

Be sure of your hose. Ask for flawless MERCURY nylons, in fashion's loveliest shades. For fine lingerie say MERCURY, too!

Among the well-dressed

...it's

MERCURY

Made exclusively at Mercury Mills Limited, Hamilton, Canada

Nylon stockings were available during World War II, but supplies were limited so women mostly wore stockings of rayon or lisle. As soon as war ended, however, they switched to nylon stockings and learned to continually check their seams to ensure they were straight. (COURTESY *CHATELAINE* MAGAZINE)

mining regions of Alberta, particularly Drumheller and Mountain Park, old-timers remembered the Syrian peddlers coming through once or twice a year with their collections of clothing, pots, pans, and other odds and ends for sale. Usually, they had corsets among their wares too, especially selected for regular customers.

Another solution was the catalogue. If Timothy Eaton hadn't come up with his first Canadian edition in 1884, someone else would have had to. It was so logical and necessary. The only problem with buying a corset from a catalogue, however, was the sizing. How do you buy a corset or a girdle from the catalogue when the sizes are simply small, medium, large, stout and sometimes extra stout? There's not much cachet or science in those descriptions. Enter the Spirella Corset Company, which decided to sell foundations in the same way as Avon products. Spirella saleswomen—corsetieres—would come to the home, measure the homemaker in complete privacy and then recommend the right garment. Confidentiality was guaranteed. Customers welcomed the idea, and it was a welcome source of cash for the local Spirella representatives.

In 1953, Ethel Taylor of Red Deer, Alberta, became a Spirella corsetiere. Her business card said, "I will show you without obligation how to look lovelier, feel younger. For the finest, smartest foundation garments, get in touch with me for an appointment." She'd have house parties, rather like the Tupperware parties of more recent years, with contests and games. Naturally, one of the favorite titles chosen for charades was the old hymn "How Firm a Foundation."

Later, her guests would contact her, and she'd go to their homes and measure them up according to the detailed computations required by the Spirella company. Off went the order, and some weeks later Taylor would be back to deliver the corset or girdle and ensure the fit. She would also assure the customer that the garment was guaranteed for one year against rust or breakage—not exactly the words you'd expect in connection with a piece of clothing. But Spirella claimed they could make such a grand statement because their stays were made of high-grade, tensile steel bent into S shapes. According to the sales claim, "It bends and twists freely in any direction."

Apparently, the guarantee held. In the Glenbow Museum in Calgary there's a letter from satisfied customer: "From experience, I can truly recommend Spirella. Gives support to my abdoman

[sic] and makes me feel so uplifted in spirits." Marguerite Schumacher of Calgary remembered that her mother also swore by Spirella. She once left her corset behind in a motel and was worried that she'd never get it back, especially since it had some money in the specially constructed pocket within the corset itself. She did get the Spirella back, and although her daughter isn't sure about the money, she is sure about the importance of that Spirella.

Spirella must have been a positive experience for Ethel Taylor too. She later went into city and provincial politics, and a major thoroughfare in Red Deer was named for her.

A Bra Is Born

In 1913 a young New York socialite was dressing to go out for the evening when she picked up two hankies, held them up over her breasts and said, "Eureka." Thus Mary Phelps Jacobs invented the bra. Or maybe it was her French maid who helped her put the two hankies together with pink ribbon so that they could be worn under her evening clothes instead of the usual heavy-duty corset.

Ms. Jacobs certainly had genes of the right kind to do it. For one thing, she must have been slender to get away with two hankies for a bra. For another, she was descended from the Fulton family whose most celebrated member was the Robert Fulton who was the first to power a boat with a steam engine. Years later she said, "I believe my ardor for invention springs from his loins. I cannot say that the brassiere will ever take as great a place in history as the steam boat but I did invent it." On the contrary, Ms. Jacobs, your invention of the brassiere was at least as important, and it has nothing to do with loins. After turning out a few copies of the brassiere for her friends, she sold the rights to the Warner Bros. Corset Company for $1,500. It should have been for millions, but who knew then?

Brassieres, or bras, didn't set the world on fire right away. Many women found their corset and camisole combination quite adequate until the 1920s, when suddenly the flapper era demanded the boyish shape—no hips, no breasts, just a long pencil-thin line. Bras had to slim down and flatten a woman's figure. No bouncing, please. We're flappers. Ten years later, when the Depression hit, a little uplift was needed in more ways than one, so bras stopped squashing and lifted a bit. Until then, they had been more like a bandeau. Now they separated. Now there were definitely two mounds.

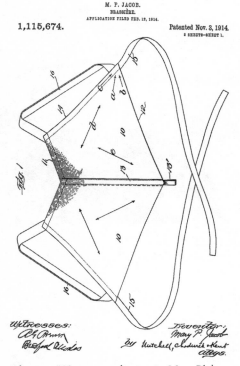

The 1914 U.S. patent application for Mary Phelps Jacobs' bra. (COURTESY WIKIPEDIA)

as it uplifts the contours

The 1930s and 1940s produced the word brassiere *and a new science to create "proud high bosoms" perfectly molded to fashion's dictates. Some wags called them little tents for the chest or mountain peaks for the unwary.*
(COURTESY *CHATELAINE* MAGAZINE)

Once mounds appeared on the scene, it became evident that not all mounds were created equal. It was necessary to identify cup sizes. Until then, one size had been supposed to fit all, though a British firm did try to differentiate somewhat with names like junior, medium, full and full with wide waist, which sounds a lot like the underwear offered in Canadian catalogues for the "stylish stout."

There were jokes about there being four cup sizes: egg cup, coffee cup, tea cup and challenge cup. But the whole issue was cleared up when someone decided on the A, B, C system, a straightforward arrangement that still exists today. A recent newspaper article said that, according to experts who know, bra sizes are growing. JJ is now the biggest size; in the early 1980s, DD was the biggest.

Howard Hughes, aeronautical engineer and movie entrepreneur, decided he'd make the most of Jane Russell in the 1941 film *The Outlaw* by designing her bra. He got out his slide rule and protractor and, with the same care and science that he put into his airplane designs, he designed a bra using the principles of cantilevering. This is a system seen in the beams projecting from a wall to support a balcony. The resulting bra was a pointy product, but the balcony held up very well and audiences could talk of nothing else.

The strapless bra came along in the late 1930s but didn't catch on until the 1950s when strapless evening gowns arrived. Put a strapless bra under a strapless gown and you had a woman who never took an easy breath all evening. But the most memorable development of the 1950s was the marketing campaign for the Maidenform brassiere with its circular stitching and pointy cups like mountain peaks. The advertisements featured women in exciting situations with text along the lines of: "I Dreamed I Climbed Mount Everest in My Maidenform Brassiere" or "I Dreamed I Starred on Broadway in my Maidenform Brassiere."

In 1964 a Canadian designer, Louise Poirier, working for a Montreal-based lingerie company, came up with a "plunge and push" technology that used a wire under each cup. What's more, she identified fifty-four elements that had to be considered when designing a bra. Who would have thought a bra could be so complicated? However, Poirier's under-wired, scientifically designed bra was such a success that the Gossard company licensed the idea and made it into a world-wide success under the trade name of Wonderbra.

While that Canadian achievement may not be as well known as maple syrup or Don Cherry, it has affected a great many Canadians, though the irony is that as soon as Louise Poirier had perfected the bra, many Canadian women gave up wearing them. Bras were suddenly a yoke of oppressive femininity and deserved to be burned. Not that anybody has been able to prove that any women actually burned their bras at the height of the women's movement, but women did doff their bras and droop through the 1970s with the braless look. But nothing lasts forever in the world of fashion.

Today, a girl's first bra isn't a very big deal. Girls are taught to be proud of their bodies and excited about the development of breasts, a reaction that is almost entirely opposite the experience of girls fifty years ago. As Kay Mullen of Olds remembered, "We weren't allowed to be proud, but we sure could be embarrassed."

Coming of age in the 1920s and 1930s wasn't too bad because bras still tried to minimize rather than maximize the attributes. This gave a girl a few months to get used to the change in profile. But girls who had to get into their first bra in the 1940s and 1950s had to deal with the spiral-stitched variety, sometimes known as the whirlpool bra, that sat like two little cone-shaped tents on a girl's

The basketball team from Grande Prairie, Alberta, in 1955 could have labeled their team picture: I Dreamed I Won the Tournament in My Maidenform Brassiere. They are Ruth Floen, Ginger Laughlin, Alice Moyer, Eloise Bode, Ardyth Hagerman, Hilda Arneson. (COURTESY GINGER KELLY)

chest. There was no way you could hide your new status.

Dawn Stephenson said about her first bra, "It was a horrible little harness," but at least she was glad to be able to finally uncross her arms and take off her jacket while at school. That's how many girls dealt with the awkward before-bra stage—by wearing cardigan sweaters or jackets and crossing their arms over their chests.

B, who asked that her name not be used, recalled that her first bra was an old one of her mother's. The cups were too big, of course, but there wasn't time to go into town just then to get her "fixed up." Why fuss over a brassiere for a kid, after all? So B's mom made a big dart in each of the cups and said that would do for now. "I was mortified, but she said I'd grow into it eventually," B remembered.

Noreen Olson's first bra, on the other hand, was pretty fancy. Called a French brassiere, it laced at the back and then tied around to the front. The trouble was that her mom made it from parachute material sent to the family by an aunt who lived in Nome, Alaska. The material was entirely suitable for a bra, and her mom was a good seamstress. But Noreen had to be careful that nobody ever saw it because it had little blue circles all over it with the words PROPERTY OF THE US NAVY. "That nylon wore forever and years later it was possible to see some member of our family in a slip or night-gown marked 'Property of the US Navy,'" she remembered.

Helen Couillard's first bra was also made of nylon, a slippery rig that kept sliding off her shoulders and down her torso. At recess, she'd have to go out and fish the thing up again. "I might as well have glued it on," she said. "It wasn't worth a darn."

Flour sacks came to the rescue yet again when Josephine Hitz got her first bra. "It was a straight piece of bleached flour-sack material gathered across the top, tucked in at the sides and front, attached at the back with a button. Nothing fancy, but it served the purpose," she recalled.

That tells it all. Bras had a purpose in days gone by. They were not fashion statements. They were support in order to present a decent and uplifted front to the world. And, by the way, don't mention them.

I See London, I See Bloomers...

In 1851, the American Amelia Bloomer put on some pants and made history. They didn't really look like pants. They were more like a baggy divided skirt that came to her ankles and were worn under yet another baggy skirt that reached below her knees. You couldn't have seen an inch of flesh if you'd tried, but they were the biggest scandal ever seen in women's clothing.

Mrs. Bloomer, a temperance reformer and advocate of women's rights, wore her "Turkish pantaloons" whenever she made a speech about women and the restrictions placed upon them. That was bad enough. But when she began writing about them and spreading the idea beyond Seneca Falls, New York, and across the Atlantic, Queen Victoria was not amused. She roundly condemned Mrs. Bloomer's ideas. Editorialists on both sides of the Atlantic predicted the end of the world if women should be so bold, the hussies. The whole idea eventually sank under ridicule and didn't come back until the 1880s when it was reintroduced under the umbrella of the Rational Dress Society.

Since the Rational Dress Society supported the bloomer dress in the name of health, and since the old Queen had just sponsored the International Health Exhibition in London, the bloomer dress slowly became respectable. Besides, there was another new player in the game: the bicycle. Women wanted it to ride to the next village, to see what was

over the hill. It was a freedom they'd never had, and if it took a pantaloon or two to get it, they were willing.

Bloomers started out as pants to be worn on the outside, more like trousers. It's not clear how that name eventually came to mean the undergarment known as bloomers. But from the early 1900s on, bloomers meant the undergarments that had formerly been known as knickers or pantaloons. In their very early stages, these had been open crotch, the theory being that women simply pulled apart the two sides of their pantaloons and went to the bathroom that way, an act that must have involved some careful rearrangement of petticoats and skirts. By the beginning of the twentieth century, however, knickers or pantaloons were mostly the closed-crotch style. The development of elastic had made it possible to pull them up and down without the complications of buttons and ribbons.

It was about this time that navy blue fleece-lined bloomers became available as warm, modest, fairly inexpensive underpants for girls. Mothers loved them. Daughters hated them. In the Grimshaw local history *Land of Hope and Dreams*, Irene McFaddin recalls: "How I hated the big navy blue bloomers we wore along with black

By 1897 Sears Roebuck was actually advertising what they called "Walking and Bicycle Suits." Legs were still under wraps, however, either under the skirt or hidden by leggings.

Misses' and Women's Winter-Weight Bloomers— They're Warm and Cosy

These are the Bloomers that are so popular for cold Winter wear. Made of sturdy Cotton with a softly brushed Fleece inner surface. Strong and serviceable elastic at waist and knees. A good weight in a nice range of colors—Navy, Grey or Peach.

19-R980. Misses' sizes: 16 to 18 years. To fit women's bust sizes: 34 to 44. .43
Price delivered, each.

19-R980X. To fit women's extra large bust sizes: 46 to 50. .53
Price delivered, each.

*The standard issue, fleece-lined bloomers, usually navy blue, the kind that so many girls hated in their school years. (*Eaton's Catalogue, fall&winter, 1929-30)

ribbed stockings and ugly black felt boots mother laced up on us."

"Bloomers? Oh, they were terrible," Doris Gilkes agreed. "So bulky for one thing. Then you had ribbed stockings to go with them, held up with elastic tied around your leg."

Lois Stanahan of Peace River also had a double load of elastic around her legs. First of all, she had purple bloomers elasticized around the leg. "They literally bloomed out around you," she remembered. Then she had to pull on long stockings and secure them with tight elastics. "By the end of winter, I had grooves in my legs," she recalled.

"How times have changed," Mary Prowse wrote in *The Spirit of Ghost Pine*, another local history book. "When I think of sleigh riding, I think of fleece-lined navy blue bloomers that dyed my long underwear beneath it." Hers was a double jeopardy—bloomers and long underwear.

Grace Budgeon's double jeopardy consisted of long stockings and long underwear, a pairing that always meant a lumpy leg line, no matter what. But Grace tried. Rather than attempt to fold and smooth the long underwear under the stockings, she'd take her stockings down when she got to school. Then she'd pull the underwear legs up and shove them into her bloomers, then pull up the stockings once more and secure them under the bloomer elastic as well. It was a heavy load for the elastic, but at least for a while she'd have a lovely smooth leg line. Others who tried to stuff their underwear under their stockings had a smooth line only on Mondays, the first day of clean—and, therefore, tight—underwear. From then on, things just got baggier and baggier as the week went on until, by Friday, the underwear could be wrapped almost double around a girl's ankle.

Consider also the elastic holding up the bloomers and stockings. It wasn't very dependable in the early days, so bloomers could lose the elastic at waist or knee without any warning. You'd be at the blackboard writing a sentence using the word *tragedy* when suddenly there'd be a ping and down would droop your bloomers. Or your stockings. Either way, you were branded for life and knew very well what the word *tragedy* meant.

No wonder girls didn't play as many active games as the boys. They had the everlasting worry of their underwear, and they always had to have a safety pin handy, attached to their shirt or perhaps the treacherous bloomers. That's another thing about growing up as a girl in the bad old days. Girls and women knew the real meaning of the word *safety* in safety pins. "Pins were one of the most valuable things you could have in the early days," Ingeborg T. said.

Then, as if navy blue bloomers hadn't been embarrassing enough, along came the Depression years and Bennett bloomers. R.B. Bennett had the bad luck to be Canada's prime minister when the 1930 depression hit the country so naturally he got the blame for the bad times. In the West, for example, people couldn't afford gas for their cars so they removed the motor and hitched the vehicle to a team of horses. It became known as the Bennett buggy, and no doubt every time the farmer and his family got behind the horses in their shell of a car they thought bitterly about Mr. Bennett.

It was the same with bloomers made from flour sacks. When money ran out and there wasn't enough even for the dreaded navy blue bloomers, women had to improvise. That's when the flour sack became one of the most important and versatile household items.

Flour in those days came in 50- or 100-pound, good-quality cotton sacks. Once the flour was used, there remained a perfectly good piece of cotton that, once the words had been removed by various methods of bleaching and boil-ing, was big enough to cut up to make necessary household items. First, it was used for tea towels and diapers. Then money got even tighter. So the flour sack moved up the rungs of respectability and was turned into blouses, clothes for the babies, and even bloomers for the women of the household. As women pulled on their stiff, bulky Bennett bloomers, they never forgave Mr. Bennett. No wonder that after his stint as prime minister of Canada he moved to England, where Bennett bloomers were unknown.

The printing on the flour sacks caused the most trouble. Sometimes mothers didn't try very hard to remove the words. After all, who was going to see them on a pair of bloomers? But inevitably, the girl who was sliding into second base would suddenly show the world that she was THE BEST IN THE WEST. Or the girl who was whirled off her feet during a square dance would show one and all that she was ROBIN HOOD'S FINEST. There are legions of stories about embarrassing moments with flour sack bloomers.

Still, without those flour sacks, there might not have been bloomers at all. During the Dirty Thirties, they were absolutely essential to the survival of families who had to make do or do without.

Mom used what was considered to be good quality cotton from sugar and flour sacks to make a lot of the things that we needed. At one point, the Wartime Prices and Trade Board announced that the cotton, sugar, and flour sacks were the property of the government and that it would be a criminal offence to damage or destroy them in any way. Mom said if they wanted their sacks back, they would have to come and take them off her children. — The Hugo story in The Spirit of Ghost Pine.

After the Depression and after the war, silk and rayon panties became more available. Some styles featured flared legs, a sign of brazen behavior, according to Grace Budgeon, but they were not likely to be hidden inside a pillowcase on the line because there was a certain secret pride in being able to afford them. Grace also told the story of an elderly woman who—having had enough of flour-sack and navy blue fleece-lined bloomers in her lifetime—sent away to Montreal for a silk undershirt and silk knee-length knickers so that she could be buried in silk.

Chapter 3
We Had Our Secrets

★   ★   ★   ★   ★

*G*RACE BUDGEON OF CROSSFIELD, ALBERTA, a feisty woman in her eighties, said as I ended my interview with her, "It's an awful thing to be born a female." As the experts in human experience would say these days, she had many issues with the way her life had turned out. Still, she was smart, brave and strong. I admired her enormously, so I wondered if her life had been all that bad. Maybe she was exaggerating.

But no. When you look at the private parts of women's lives, all the hidden parts that nobody ever talked about years ago, she was right. As a woman, you had to menstruate, have intercourse, carry and bear children until your body shut down, then live through menopause—all the while being cheerful about it and quiet. Especially quiet. There was to be no mention of the personal issues of a woman's life. That was private. That was nobody's business and woe betide the woman who broke those rules and dared to ask for help. Birth control advice? Don't ask. A doctor when the baby comes? Good luck. Intelligent discussion about the female body and its problems? Figure it out for yourself.

So why didn't women object? Why did they put up with the silences and lack of services?

Because it wasn't proper to object. Because permission had not yet been granted to talk about the lives of women. Because there wasn't time. Because women were isolated by distance and language. Because there was no money. Because women felt it was their lot in life to suffer, and many men thought so too. Because, because.

Take, for instance, this story of one woman's life in *No Streets of Gold* by Helen Potrebenko.

Most of my mother's days were spent in the harsh drabness of labor. Day after day after day she kept lifting and bending and carrying. But when you write about someone's life, you write of the highs and lows, not the dullness of unceasing labor. It's not that she worked all that fast . . . the work in pre-industrial societies wasn't done at such a speed or under such pressure. But it was more difficult, more boring, more endless, and never resulted in anything observable except survival.

Except survival. As if there were anything else. Survive. That's what many of the first women in the West had to do: just keep putting one foot in front of the other to survive.

There's the story of Louise and Henry. After fighting overseas in World War I, Henry, who had grown up in the Hull area of Quebec, came back to Canada and decided to head for northern Alberta, where he had heard there were settlements of French Canadian homesteaders. On his way across Canada, a Catholic priest came through the train looking for someone who could speak French. Henry volunteered his help and met eighteen-year-old Louise, who had also grown up in Quebec. She was headed for Saskatchewan to live with a married sister who didn't really want her. So Henry and Louise made a deal. They'd be married at the very next stop. This is not a romantic story of love at first sight. This is strictly business. Henry needed a wife, Louise needed a home. Years later she told her son, "He looked like a good man. He needed a wife and I needed somebody to look after me as I had no place to go."

Did she know anything about marriage, about birth control, about childbirth? Not likely. Her mother was dead. Louise was on her own in more ways than one. What did it feel like to be so alone in a strange land with a strange husband? Not that it mattered what it felt like. There was no help available anyway. Live or die. Sink or swim. Don't whine.

Elaine Leslau Silverman, in her book

The Last Best West, said that girls and women learned "to play parts in scripts they had not written." They learned to be silent about their lives, keep things private, never ask questions. Or as one woman told me, "We took what we got because we couldn't do anything about it anyway."

Not all the stories in this chapter are as extreme as those. There were women who got through their lives gently and happily, often with humor. But underneath the brave talk there was generally a recognition that it was sometimes hard to be female. Some wished they had known more, asked more, given more to their own daughters. That was a frequent lament. We (for I'm just as guilty here) didn't always do a good job of explaining the unmentionable subjects to our own children. It's not easy to shuck off the training of our mothers and grandmothers, even in this brave new world when every unmentionable is being mentioned over and over again. Some women I talked with actually said they wished the word *unmentionables* could be brought back and acted upon. "Is there no end to what we have to uncover and mention now?" they asked.

But maybe uncovering is good for us. Maybe it brings about understanding and that overused word *closure.* Maybe uncovering helps to explain some of the enormous changes we've lived through in the last hundred years, or twenty years, or even the last two years. Change is changing faster than ever. But I begin to sound like my mother, so I won't carry on about change. I'll just uncover some stories of the unmentionable parts of women's private lives in the past, all those things our mothers wouldn't tell us.

Aboriginal Women and the Questions Never Asked

Canada's first women, the women of the First Nations, had to deal with being female just like every other woman before or since. They had menstrual periods, they had sex, they had babies, they had menopause. It was all there, the whole messy business. So how did they manage?

We are not told much. The male fur traders and explorers who first ventured into the West didn't think to ask the women about their underwear and other related unmentionable subjects. That was probably a good thing, since the aboriginals had their own sense of modesty and such subjects would have been off limits. There's also the problem of language. How would you say to a First Nations chief, "And does your wife wear panties?" It would not be proper.

There is a lot of talk, however, about moss. Mostly, it's assumed that the moss is gathered for use as babies' diapers. Sylvia Van Kirk in *Many Tender Ties*—the best book anywhere about aboriginal women and children—quotes J.H. LeFroy, who visited the West in the mid-1800s. He describes an Indian cradle:

> The outside case is made of cloth . . . and embroidery . . . the inside stuffing is a soft silky moss, very abundant in this country, so that nothing can be so economical.

Well, if moss works for babies, why not for women during their menstrual periods? Van Kirk also mentions a voyageur at Fort Chipewyan who was observed helping his wife collect moss. The report of this action got back to headquarters because other men at the post thought it was unmanly of him to fetch and carry for an aboriginal woman. But why did the woman need moss? For the baby? Yes, but could there be something else? George Simpson, never one to show much concern for women, may have supplied a clue when he wrote a rebuke to one of his traders for bringing along his wife and children when he could have been carrying furs

in their place. Don't let delays happen, he scolded, in order to carry women and children in the canoes with "their Baggage Pots Pans Kettles and Bags of Moss." That's another mention of moss. Surely, that's what women were using for their periods. But in winter? How did aboriginal women get moss when the rivers and sloughs were frozen solid?

Beverly Hungry Wolf, who describes herself as a member of the Blood tribe of the Blackfeet, has the answer. Moss was used for menstrual periods as well as for babies' diapers and bedding, she recalled. They stockpiled the moss during summer months and took it with them as they traveled, or they knew where to find moss hanging on trees near river banks during the winter months. If it was frozen, they melted it and then dried it for use. She remembered her aunt, Mary One Spot, hanging moss in trees alongside a river one summer day, there to dry and eventually be packed into bags for use over the winter.

In her book *The Ways of My Grandmothers*, Hungry Wolf also recalls that her foremothers sometimes used "woman's sage" during menstrual periods. This is a bushy prairie plant with a sharp taste and smell. According to Hungry Wolf, to keep the moss or sage close to the body, it would have been held with a piece of leather, rather like an apron that folded from front to back and was secured close to the body by leather thongs. As she explained in her later book, *Daughters of the Buffalo Women,* "Back then they always saved the thickest and softest pieces of tanned hide and they cut these sort of like a small apron and that is what they used during their monthly periods. When it was soiled, a girl or woman would go off by herself and she would lay it out and let it dry, then after that she would scrape it clean with a rough rock so she could put it back on again."

In the Blood tradition, according to Hungry Wolf, a girl's first period was a time for celebration. She'd be required to live in seclusion for four days, after which the women of the community met to bless her and exchange gifts in a coming-of-age ceremony. And from then on, whenever she got her period, she'd be expected to rest a bit more, to isolate herself from the community somewhat, not because it was a shameful thing she was doing, but because it was a holy time in her cycles. Beverly's grandfather, Pat Weaselhead, explained that men had to take sweat baths to cleanse themselves, but women were cleansed during menstruation. Therefore, a woman was holiest during her period,

powerful almost, which is why she would be excused from some of the usual duties.

Beverly Hungry Wolf herself didn't get a coming-of-age ceremony upon her first period because she was in a residential school by that time. The nuns simply gave her a bag of sanitary pads, told her not to stain the sheets, and left explanations up to the older girls in the dorm.

Ellen Smallboy, a Cree woman from northern Manitoba, didn't have a ceremony upon her first menstrual period either. Instead, she nearly died. She fell out of a canoe when she was about fifteen years old. "Nobody knew how to swim in those days. I kept (afloat) for about a mile and it seemed as if it was very dark," she remembered. "I washed up on a little dry earth on the shore. I had nothing on but my dress. After I got home, I started menstruating." Not that she would have used the actual word *menstruating.* Cree girls were taught to refer to this stage in a woman's life as "the fox has bitten you" or "your grandmother has come to you."

The Prairie Maternity Ward

First Nations women gave birth wherever and whenever—which isn't to say they didn't prepare and take care. They did. Childbirth was not a reason to shut down. It was a woman's thing, and women were expected to manage it without too much fuss from the mother-to-be or from those helping her. When labor became pronounced, the pregnant woman would move to her own tent and then kneel or squat over a low object. Sometimes, she'd have a pole to grasp, and in that position would push the baby out. This makes sense, in that she's working with gravity, not against it. She'd stay in that position until the afterbirth came as well.

Even if the baby was born on a bed, the custom was to have the mother get up and squat at this point in order to expel the placenta. Beverly Hungry Wolf quotes a Blackfoot Nation woman who remembered her sister's first baby.

> When the time finally arrived for the baby to come out, that old lady [the aboriginal midwife] again sang her song, then suddenly the baby just came out. Right after that, she told my sister to kneel, then she held her tight around the middle of her waist and she kept rubbing downward until the afterbirth was out. . . . My sister was put on a bed afterwards with a pillow at each end but that old lady wouldn't let her

lay still for too long, nor go to sleep. There were a couple of old women there with her all night, brewing a big pot of coffee and making her drink some to stay awake. There was still blood inside her; they kept her moving around so that it wouldn't coagulate.

Babies weren't considered "alive" until they'd lived for thirty days, at which time they'd be taken to the elders to be named. At the same time, the mother would move her camp, get new clothes and get on with her life.

The men "from away," the traders and explorers, were amazed at the strength of these women, including the strength they demonstrated in childbirth. One wrote that a woman in his company during a journey simply dropped behind the company, then brought forth "the little stranger," tied it into a cradle board and carried on with the trip. Could it be, the white men wondered, that their wives back in England carried on a bit too much, staying in bed for a full month after birth and generally making childbirth a big deal?

George Barker, in his book *Forty Years a Chief*, quoted his grandmother expressing the opinion that women were strong, but especially so during childbirth. She and his grandfather were moving to a different reserve in mid-winter when she went into labor. Grandfather went off looking for poles to construct the teepee, and when he got back, his wife had delivered the child, a baby boy, herself. She used snow to wash him off, she told her grandson many years later, and even though the newborn shivered and cried with the cold, he was fine as soon as he was wrapped into his cradle board. His grandmother always believed that her son was particularly strong and able to withstand extreme cold all through his life because of his first bath in snow.

Of course, not every birth story ended so happily. Some babies died in the first few days and months of their lives, as did the women who bore them. It is interesting to note that aboriginal women seemed able to space their families. For one thing, they breast fed for a long time, a practice that is thought by some to prevent pregnancy. Certain women were thought to know the native plants and herbs that worked as contraceptives or caused abortion. Still others were said to have the spiritual power to "tie" women so they'd never have children again.

Once aboriginal women married fur traders and lived a more "civilized" life, they seemed to have more difficult deliveries and more children. The average number of children for a woman in Cree society was four; the average for the country wife of a trader was eight to twelve. Sylvia Van Kirk offers three factors for the larger families: a better diet, less hard, grinding work, and the loss of traditional sexual taboos. The white men who married in the fashion of the country had no such taboos, and the winters were long and cold.

The Birds and the Bees: Who Knew Anything about Them?

Alexa Church, a ninety-five-year-old pioneer of western Canada and the survivor of many challenges throughout her lifetime, wasn't shocked by my question about sex, but she was surprised. Women of her generation didn't talk about such things. Still, when I asked her how she had learned about the birds and bees so many years ago, she took a deep breath, thought about it and then said, "It must have come on the wind, I guess." Like so many women of the early 1900s, she figured it out for herself.

In 1905 Catherine Neil came from Scotland to Medicine Hat, Alberta, to be married to her childhood friend, now a sheep rancher in southern Alberta. She got off the train one day, married her Jim the next day and headed off to

"Girls were not allowed to go out into the barnyard when the neighbor brought the cows to be impregnated, and when my baby sister was about to be born at home, dad took me to a neighbor so that I wouldn't hear the sounds of birth." —Aurelia Vangrud

the ranch. "I was an only girl and had been raised by one of those reserved Scots mothers who think it is time enough for a girl to learn things about married life after they are married—always in the hope that she will be at hand to tell a young wife all she should know." But Catherine's mother was not nearby. Catherine had to learn about a man and married life on her own.

There was no such thing as sex education in school. A teacher would have been run out of the county if he or she had tried to explain sex. It was not to be spoken of. The students in a rural school in the Peace River region of Alberta knew the teacher was getting into dangerous territory when he began to blush and leave out whole passages of the Zane Grey book he was reading aloud to them. "We knew there was something there we were missing, but we didn't know what," Karen Burgess remembered years later. It was their first sex education—not that Zane Grey ever got very sexy.

In later years, schools offered a course called Health and Personal Development. The picture of organs in a girl's body ended at her stomach. End of story. Don't ask. Yet in spite of themselves, schools were the source of most sex education in early days. The

girls would tell the girls, the boys would tell the boys and neither knew anything.

That's pretty much what happened with Maggie Gilkes when she was about eleven:

I was riding to school one day with my girlfriend. All of a sudden she stopped her horse and said, "Do you know what f—u—c—k means?" She spelled it out so I asked, "What's fuck?" and she said, "Sshh, you're not supposed to say it." Then she told me how babies were conceived. I don't know why I didn't know. I'd seen the cattle breed all the time, but I didn't connect it with humans. I was absolutely shocked by it. I looked at my parents quite differently. Everything changed right then.

Some homes had doctor books. Phyllis Robinson of Calgary found their family doctor book hidden on a shelf behind a trunk in the dark passageway to the basement. So she read up on the subject, figured out what goes where, but could never figure out why. There was no hint that there might be an emotional component to the whole mechanical process. Dawn Stephenson also found the doctor book. "Couldn't make head nor tail of the thing," she said, "but the pictures were interesting."

Kay Hurlburt worked in her uncle's drugstore, and there she too found books. They were carefully wrapped in brown paper so she had to unwrap and wrap them up again so that no one would know she'd been peeking. It wasn't worth the trouble, she decided.

How they extracted information from some of these so-called doctor books is a good question. Mary Ries Melendy, MD, PhD, author of scientific works and an eminent practitioner (according to the publisher's blurb) says this in her 1904 book *Vivilore: The Pathway to Mental and Physical Perfection:* "Love's alphabet teaches the pleasure of harmonious sex relations and that children often result from the mere physical union, with or without recognition of the higher powers." Figure that one out, if you can!

Here's what Dr. J.H. Kellogg in *The Home Book of Modern Medicine* (1914) says about the same subject:

As has been previously observed, in all except the very lowest forms of life, two elements are necessary to the production of a new individual or a reproduction of the species—a male element and a female element. The special organs by means of which these elements are produced, brought together, and developed into the new individual in a more or less perfect state are termed sexual organs.

Every school really should have had medical books just lying around for students to dip into at random. It might have encouraged them to read, to learn some new words and to give up any idea of sex forever.

Mothers were supposed to look after this part of a girl's education, but they weren't too good at it. Lois Shanahan of Peace River asked her mom about the facts of life when she was eleven. "I'll tell you all about it when you're thirteen," her mother said. But Lois menstruated before she was thirteen so the story had to come out. By that time, Lois had read some books, better ones than those most girls read, and had a pretty good idea of what was happening. "I probably knew as much as my mother did so we never really discussed it," Lois recalled. "She certainly didn't explain the technique of making babies. These things embarrassed her."

They embarrassed most mothers. Jacy Moore's mother in Grande Prairie outlined the process as briefly as possible and then told her daughter to watch out for "cheap thrills." Whatever they were.

When babies came to the Bellavance family of Radville, Saskatchewan, the older children were told that some Indians had come by while they were at school and forced their mother to take a baby they didn't want. The children bought the story—for a while at least. Another family blamed the Eaton's catalogue for the new baby in their midst: it came in the mail.

In fact, the booklets produced by Kotex starting in the 1930s, *Are You In the Know?* and *Very Personally Yours,* were likely used more often than any other form of sex education. Laurie Stefaniuk's mom gave her one of these pamphlets to read, then took her for a walk and said, "Do you have any questions?" Laurie said no, and that was the end of that conversation. Many mothers took the easy way out and simply left one of the booklets on the dresser to help their daughters understand "things." The booklets explained menstruation well, but when it came to sex, they were no help at all.

What girls needed was Josephine Hitz's aunt. "How do you make babies?" thirteen-year-old Josephine asked her one day. "The man puts his thing in you and that makes a baby," her aunt replied. Years later, Josephine remembered how she thought that was a bit much. "I didn't know you had to go through all that performance."

It was the kissing that did it, according to one of Prue Penley's school chums. If you wanted a baby, you kissed in a certain way. She wasn't sure of the technique, but the information certainly discouraged kissing for a while.

Betty Putters got a straightforward explanation:

When I was twelve in 1947, I went to a CGIT [Canadian Girls in Training] camp at Lake Wabumun. One night the nurse sat us all down and started with the basics and carried us right on through to procreation. She didn't use the banana and the condom as they do in today's Grade Four classes. I think I surprised my mom by actually knowing more about the whole process than she did.

When Beverly Hungry Wolf asked her mother the dreaded question, "How do babies come?" her mother gave her the dreaded answer: "When the time comes, you'll find out about it." This was in the 1960s on the Blood reserve of southern Alberta. But it could have been one hundred or even six hundred years earlier. Keeping your girls innocent was thought to be the right thing to do. Not just on reserves but throughout any part of the world connected to Great Britain.

According to Helen Potrebenko, two tough, realistic twelve-year-old girls learned one day about the facts of life from other girls at school. Since they were both the oldest in very large families and had a lot of responsibility and work for the younger children, they went home and told their mothers to cut out this baby making activity. They'd had enough.

I Thought I Was Going to Die

There is no mention of women and their menstrual periods in the accounts of life and times in the early settlement of the West, and it's not entirely due to the fact that menstruation was a female thing and nobody's business. Menstruation was somehow shameful, a curse settled upon women for being born female. Why? Who knew? But it meant that girls learned early on that they had to be silent about their monthly passage and carry on the tradition of silence and shame.

Freda McCann was five years old and playing under her mom and dad's bed

in war-time London when she noticed a lot of wet cloths strung through the coils of the bed springs. Her mother wouldn't tell her what they were, of course. But years later, the light went on when Freda realized they had been the cloths her mother used for menstrual periods. They were such a shameful sight, apparently, that her mother couldn't hang them outside on the line, drape them over the fence or even on a line in the house. They had to go under the bed in the dark. That's what menstruation was—a black hole, not to be named. That's why it went by various coy terms such as "wearing the rag" and "falling off the roof."

Like Freda's mother, most women made their own pads, either with rags left from old towels and sheets, or with new material such as flannel and cheesecloth available from stores and catalogues. The 1925 Eaton's catalogue listed Eatonia Absorbent Cotton, "very absorbent and clean and . . . sterilized . . . free from all infection." One pound sold for seventy-five cents. Household gauze, pictured right next to the cotton, is "for general use around the home, such as making pads, cleaning, etc." and sold for thirty-nine cents.

The cotton would be cut and folded into the right width and length for a

By 1928, Chatelaine *Magazine featured the "shadow skirt" and "shadow step-in," both of which were intended to prevent staining one's clothes during a menstrual period. These good ideas seem to have disappeared from catalogues and magazines after Kotex and Modess began their major advertising campaigns.*

pad, then wrapped in the gauze to hold it together. The cotton was washable and could be reused, making home-made pads much cheaper than store-bought. The same Eaton's catalogue advertised Kotex pads, a box of twelve for sixty-nine cents—a lot of money in 1925. All across western Canada, menstrual cloths must have been hanging on many a clothesline or under many a bed. But did anybody see them? No. It was the height of shame to be caught with your menstruation showing.

Women from European countries sometimes crocheted or knitted menstrual pads. These, of course, had to be washed after each use, so there must have been little pieces of unmentionable handiwork hanging on clotheslines too.

As for the belts to hold the pads, they were often homemade and depended a lot on pins. However, if you searched catalogues carefully, you could find a "sanitary apron." This was a rectangular piece of cloth-covered rubber that held the pad in place and then folded up around the body like a diaper. It sounds rather awkward, but it had the advantage of being rubber, which prevented staining of clothing.

Sears also offered a traveling kit that included a simple apron, several washable pads, a belt and a waterproof pouch to carry the used pads. These would be washed later or perhaps burned in a stove or fireplace. Disposing of used pads was another problem that had to be handled with great care. No wonder a woman stayed home through her monthlies.

Most older women can remember their first period. It was not presented, as it is now, as a time to rejoice in one's womanhood. It was a time to be ashamed and slink around for four or five days every month, hoping you didn't have blood on the back of your clothes. "I got my period between twelve and thirteen," Dawn Stephenson recalled. "I pinned the cloths all wrong. I had to walk funny to keep them in place because I only had those small gold pins. Practically pinned them to my skin to keep them in place. I felt like everybody knew. It was a thoroughly miserable business."

Linda Abercrombie was at camp when her first period came. "I didn't know what to do with the stained panties so I filled them with rocks and threw them into the creek." Phyllis Kane buried her stained panties.

Marjorie Norris was twelve when she began. Her mother took her into a bedroom, gave her a box of Kotex and showed her how to work the harness. Then she said, "Stay away from boys."

That was the end of that mother-daughter bonding.

"I thought I was going to die," Josephine Hitz remembered about getting her first period when she was thirteen. "I was riding a horse when all of a sudden my clothes got all bloody. Mother said, 'Every girl gets this.'" From then on, Josephine knew why there was a pail of water outside with rags in it. Her pads, also known as "diapers" in her household, were made of old flannelette sheets.

When Betty Garbutt was about six years old, she asked her mother when she was going to turn into a boy. As far as she was concerned, boys had the better time of it and she wanted to be one. However, her mother said, "Never—you're a girl. Get used to it." So she did. But when this business of being a girl suddenly included menstrual periods, she was once again ready to be a boy. "I was on a bus going to Red Deer, and on the way the bus stopped, I forget where, and I went to the bathroom. I had the curse, wouldn't you know, the first time. I knew it was coming, but why then? I had nothing with me except the old toilet paper in the bus depot bathroom, that waxy old stuff. So I stuffed that inside my panties. When I got to Red Deer, my mother's friend got the right equipment, and I carried on being a girl. The worst part was I thought I'd have this business until I died."

It did seem as if the first menstrual period often picked the very worst time to make its appearance. Lois Stranahan was in the school outhouse when she realized she had a spot of blood on the back of her skirt. Somehow she had to sidle back into her classroom without anyone noticing, grab her coat, sling it around her waist, tell the teacher she wasn't well and then tear home. That coat trick was a favorite. Many girls learned to leave it on the back of the school desk rather than hanging it in the hallway, just in case they got their first period—or their ninety-first long after school days were over. Precautions were always necessary.

The nuns at the convent school had to help Helene Couillard with her first period. None of the younger girls had been told to bring pads and a belt with them "just in case," so the nuns gave them their personal supplies until the girls' folks could send or bring what was needed. The only word that was used in the process was "outfit." The girls got an outfit, meaning the belt and pads. There was no explanation of what this meant. "Put on your outfit and say your prayers," the nuns told them. "We had no

idea what was going on," Couillard said.

In fact, the old doctor books may not be far wrong, even though their prose is a bit overdone. Dr. J.H. Kellogg, in his *Home Book of Modern Medicine*, says, "The first occurrence of menstruation is a very critical period in the life of a female, and each recurrence of the function renders her especially susceptible to morbid influences and serious derangements." Many women would agree. That first menstrual period, and all the subsequent ones, did leave one susceptible to morbid thoughts and serious derangements such as: Why wasn't I born a boy?

Even after marriage, some girls didn't realize the significance of the menses. A Cree woman who was promised to a man she'd never seen remembered in later years that she mostly cried during her marriage ceremony, cried when she was told she'd have to leave her family and live with his, cried when she saw his home, cried when her mother-in-law said she'd have to sleep with her new husband. "And when my husband would move closer, I would kick him and push him away, for I did not know him."

Eventually, she must have "known him," for she said to her mother-in-law one day, "I wonder what is the matter with me. I have not had it which I should have every month." When she heard she was to have a baby, she was amazed. "I did not know anything because in those days the old people used to guard the girls so closely; you never went anywhere."

The Wedding Night Under the Bed

If menstruation was a surprise to many girls, so was intercourse. This sex thing was somehow so shameful that the words wouldn't come out of the mouths of mothers, father and other adults. They'd just let a girl get married, with or without a lot of ceremony, and leave her to figure it out. Fairy tales do great damage with that inevitable last line, "And they lived happily ever after." As if a wedding ceremony was all it took.

Fast forward to the wedding night. What about that first experience between a man and a woman? Of course, this is now a very old-fashioned question. These days, a man and a woman have more than likely had that first experience long before their wedding night. But in the old days, it was a very big deal indeed. And entirely unmentionable—though with houses and tents being as small as many were, it's a wonder youngsters didn't learn from what they heard in their parents' bed. Maybe boys put two and two together, since they had more barnyard experience and talked more among themselves. But many girls seemed ignorant of their fate.

Mrs. X., who requested that her name not be used, a Peace River old-timer, said that she knew nothing about sex when she married. She and her new husband went to bed after the wedding dance and she went to sleep. Pretty soon she was awakened. "What are you doing?" she asked. "We're married," he said. "So what?" she said, and then she felt something that hadn't been there before. Her new husband, a kind man, explained what was expected of her. "It was when he told me what he was going to do with it that I couldn't believe my ears."

"It" didn't happen that night. But this was a Catholic union. Women were expected to obey their husbands, so she did, and they lived happily ever after, just as the fairy tales say. "He was patient," she said years later, the first time she had ever told her story.

Another woman of her acquaintance spent her wedding night under the bed rather than succumb to what awaited her in the bed above. When she went to the priest for advice, he reminded her about the word *obey* in her marriage vows. She obeyed.

In 1920 eighteen-year-old Madeleine Bird was married in Fort Chipewyan,

Northwest Territories. She'd been a student in a Catholic residential school for years, an innocent if ever there was one, and painfully shy. After her wedding dance, she followed her mother home, not her husband. Why? She didn't know the man she had married, knew nothing about the meaning of marriage and, as it turned out, her mother wasn't about to tell her right then. Her mother simply sent her to her husband's home. "I was so embarrassed to undress in front of him in the same room, alone. . . . I felt like running away back home to my mother again. I hurried to undress behind a chair, jumped in bed and faced the wall. He said, 'Are you going to sleep facing the wall tonight?' I didn't say a word but just covered up and stayed that way. But the second night, he said, 'We don't sleep like that when we are husband and wife,' and so I had to obey him."

"My mother didn't know anything about the facts of life when she got married, and she didn't tell me anything either," Madeleine wrote years later.

Doctor books weren't much help either. Take the book written in the late 1800s by J.B. Keswick with the ambitious title of *Woman, Her Physical Culture & Including Her Dress, Habits,* *Womanhood and Her Diseases and How to Cure Them.* Keswick was identified as a phrenologist, author, publisher and hydropathic practitioner, none of which indicated he was a trained doctor. But he certainly wrote as if he were. His books sold very well, some of them coming to Canada with emigrants from the British Isles. So Keswick lived on in western history.

He's not too bad when he urges mothers to educate both their daughters and their sons about women's cycles. But when he gets into the philosophy behind his advice, he ascends into the most purple of prose:

> Such knowledge would add grace to Manhood and Womanhood; it would beautify and elevate the relation and intercourse of the sexes; it would bind man to woman in a tender, holier union; it would consecrate woman in the estimate of man, and endear man to woman as a truer nobler being in all relations.

Then, after those big words, he tackles the business of self-abuse.

> It saps the foundation of womanhood, steals the flush of health

from the cheek of girlhood, and even the rosy complexion of childhood succumbs to its ravages, and a greenish hue is diffused over the face, the ruby lips lose their freshness and sweetness, the ears become pale as marble, the eyes which have outshone the diamond in brilliancy now roll languidly in their sockets and are dull and sunken and in some cases surrounded by purplish circles.

Boys used to be told that they'd go blind if they masturbated. By the sounds of it, girls and women go green, though it's hard to make head or tail of what he's talking about. Then Keswick spends a fair amount of time on the difference between passion and love. Passion is all very well, he says, but it's a weak indulgence usually exhibited by husbands, a mere gratification of selfish desires. On the other hand, love is tender and noble, love can wait with Christian forbearance until the wife can "with safety and exultation, take charge of the germ of the child and naturally develop it into life." Did you understand that to "take charge of the germ," you have to have intercourse?

A health manual published in Canada in the late 1800s was *Search Lights on Health,*

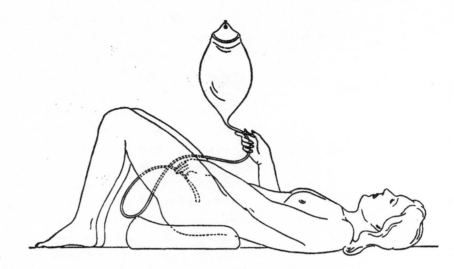

DIRECTIONS FOR TAKING A DOUCHE

1. Lie flat on the back on a bedpan or in the bathtub. The hips should be raised and the shoulders low. If the douche is taken in a sitting or semi-sitting position the water escapes almost as soon as it enters.

2. Use a fountain syringe with a glass or hard-rubber nozzle having a blind end and openings at the sides. Unless otherwise directed by me do not use a bulb syringe, for if improperly used there is danger of forcing fluid beyond the mouth of the uterus.

3. Do not hang the douche-bag more than 2 feet above the level of the bed or tub; otherwise the pressure may be excessive.

4. Use boiled water as hot as possible. Never use cold water.

5. Boil the syringe and nozzle before using.

6. Control the flow so that two quarts will take 10-15 minutes to flow through.

7. Do not use hot douche just before, during, nor just after menstrual period.

This picture was folded up inside an old doctor book in the Glenbow Museum Collection. There's no date. The woman is giving herself a douche, whether for cleanliness or birth control is not indicated.

Light on Dark Corners by B.G. Jefferis and J.L. Nichols. It too counsels self-control and absolutely no monkey business. For instance, the male "organ," as they so delicately refer to it, "was made for a high and holy purpose, and woe be to him who pollutes his manhood by practicing the secret vice." As for lovemaking, the writers recommend intercourse between a properly married man and wife about once a week or maybe every ten days. Also, intercourse should not occur just before or after meals or after mental excitement or physical exercise. Nor should intercourse occur when the husband is under the influence of alcoholic stimulants "for idiocy and other serious maladies are liable to be visited upon the offspring."

There's no end to the dire warnings in the old medical literature. *The Canadian Practitioner* of 1886 solemnly announced that a girl baby is produced when the father is in a higher state of excitement than the mother, and a boy baby when vice versa. A woeful fate is seen for the woman who tries to escape her sexuality and remain a virgin. That will bring down upon her all sorts of dire consequences. After all, "Woman exists for the womb," as one health manual of the 1890s emphasized.

Birth Control? Good Luck!

A girl figures out how to deal with menstruation. In the fullness of time, she meets a man, marries him and experiences sexual intercourse. But what if she doesn't want a baby right away? If it's 1969 or later, she's fine. That's the year that birth control became legal in Canada. Before that it was against the Criminal Code of Canada.

Section 179 of the Criminal Code, passed in 1892, states:

> Everyone is guilty of an indictable offense and liable to two years imprisonment who knowingly without lawful excuse or justification offers to sell, advertises, publishes an advertisement of or has for sale or disposal any medicine, drug or article intended or represented as a means of preventing conception or causing abortion.

The law meant that there were no legal means by which a woman could control her reproductive capacity. Doctors might be able to advise her about safe cycles, they might suggest that her husband buy condoms—not for the purpose of contraception but for "the prevention of disease." They might even perform the occasional abortion under the name of treating "menstrual irregularities." But they could not prescribe anything having to do with birth control. Not that there was anything much to prescribe, since it was illegal to sell any product that specifically identified itself as a birth control method.

Did those early women then lie down and die? Yes, a lot of them did because you can't go on having babies years after year without doctors around, without money and without help. So they died.

They also lied. One creative woman used to say to her husband as he prepared to go to bed, "You just go ahead, dear. I want to finish up this row of knitting." By the time she finished, he'd be asleep. About the five children she had, she said, "I ran out of wool sometimes. Sexy nightgowns were put into the bottom drawer in favor of flannelette, not just for the sake of warmth but also as a birth control measure.

Some women took matters in their own hands by inserting something into their vagina to prevent the transmission of the sperm. In old catalogues from the 1920s and 1930s, you'll find small sponges advertised for "cleansing" purposes. If these were soaked in a soapy solution or vinegar, then inserted into the vagina before intercourse, they sometimes worked. You had to know the language. These "sanitary sponges for ladies" were described in an advertisement for various medical items:

The above picture is the exact size of one of our soft silk netted sponges when perfectly dry. When moistened, it expands about one-half more than shown. These are extensively used by ladies when immersed in a good antiseptic and inserted well up into the vagina, the passage is kept germ free.

The word "germ" is code for "sperm," it is thought.

In journalist Violet McNaughton's personal papers is this recipe for a concoction to be used as a suppository in the vagina. It came from one of McNaughton's correspondents who said it had worked for dozens of her friends. But of course McNaughton didn't publish it in her newspaper column. She couldn't. Any talk of birth control was still illegal.

In a sauce pan over hot water, combine 1 lb. cocoa butter, 1 oz. of common boric acid and 1 1/2 oz. tannic acid [a powder like boric acid, but yellowish in color]. Melt the cocoa butter and stir it all together. Pour ½ inch thick in a pie pan and cool. Then cut into ½ inch squares like fudge and insert one piece up there when needed and it will melt and provide protection.

In the 1930s Grace Budgeon used spermicidal suppositories as well, but hers were from the drugstore. While she may have been liberated enough to decide she wasn't going to let nature take its course in her marriage, she still couldn't buy the suppositories herself. Her husband had to do that. He also bought condoms—"safes" as they were known then. It was his job to make the purchase, and he wasn't a bit embarrassed, she said. Grace also used a douche, and when asked what a douche was like, she said, "Oh, a douche was something like a grease gun."

Douches were used after intercourse, but you had to be quick and get water up there to flush out the "germs" before any damage was done. That's why douches were not a very effective birth control measure and were used more often as a cleansing agent. That's how suppositories were sold as well, under the claim they were for "deep cleansing."

Condoms were probably the most common and effective of all the birth control measures before the pill. But they had to be labeled "for the prevention of disease," and that description had to be clearly stated on the packaging. As far as women were concerned, there were three problems with condoms: You had to have some money, you had to live near a drugstore and you had to find a man who'd actually buy them. Thelma Levy remembered that her new husband was so embarrassed to go into the drug store to get the safes that he had to have a long drink of water to calm himself down first.

It took Jimmy Gilkes a while to get over the embarrassment of buying condoms after he and Doris were married, but she argued that all men should use them. "Get over it," she told him. So he did. But if the clerk in the drugstore was a woman, he'd come back later.

Sue Johanson, host of the *Sunday Night Sex Show*, tells the story of her nursing training at St. Boniface Hospital in Winnipeg, where the nuns told the trainees to poke holes in condoms "to give the sperm a fighting chance." That would be "Vatican roulette," a term that Phyllis Robinson first heard in nursing school as well.

Meanwhile, back in the drugstore, the operators had their own problems. Ken Penley of Penley Drugs in Calgary wondered why only strangers bought condoms at his drugstore. After all, the condom market was a significant one. Where were his regular customers? It turned out that they were off at some other drugstore where they wouldn't be known—because, of course, you couldn't let your friend know you were buying condoms. Penley Drugs eventually went into the mail-order business and sold a lot more condoms that way.

Every effort was made in the drugstore to hide the transaction. Condom packages were wrapped and kept in a separate drawer. Men could point to the drawer and leave their money on the counter without exchanging a word. Some who were in the know would place three fingers on the counter and the clerk (a man, of course) would know what they were asking for. That worked very well until one day a woman placed three fingers on the counter. Penley gave her a package of condoms and she gasped, "I wanted a three-cent stamp, please."

Lacking a neighborhood drugstore, some people made their own condoms. This is an 1824 recipe for condoms made from sheep gut:

Soak sheep intestines in water for some hours, turn them inside out and soak again in a weak alkaline solution. Change the solution every twelve hours. Then scrape carefully to remove the mucous membrane, leaving the peritoneal and muscular coats exposed to the vapor of burning brimstone. Now wash with soap and water, scent with essence if possible, blow the intestines up, dry them, cut to lengths of seven to eight inches, border at the end with a riband.

As tempting as it is to laugh at that recipe, there must have been women in western Canada in the 1800s who would have been happy to make such condoms, complete with riband, if their husbands would agree to use them. If it meant there'd be six kids instead of sixteen, it was well worth doing.

Even Casanova, supposedly the greatest of all romantic lovers, allegedly used condoms in his conquest of women. According to researchers at the "Hall of Contraception," a website devoted to the subject, his condoms would have been made of fine linen strips sewed together to make a tidy pouch which would be held onto the organ by a ribbon or string. It sounds a bit painful but no worse than what women in the 1500s were advised to use as contraceptives that consisted of a paste of ground dates, acacia (a tree bark) and honey that was to be inserted into the vagina on a piece of wool.

Other solutions inserted into the vagina in past centuries to keep the sperm at bay included elephant and crocodile dung held in place by some sort of pessary. Dung should do it all right. (A pessary is a ring inserted into the vagina to hold the womb in place, or to hold the solution or sheath that is supposed to keep the sperm at bay.)

Two other methods of birth control used in the old days were coitus interruptus and abstinence. They weren't known by such direct names, of course. When Josephine Hitz announced that she was going to be married, the woman she worked for decided to give her some valuable advice. "Just remember," she said, "that if you don't want a baby, get the train out of the station in the nick of time, like the NAR [Northern Alberta Railway]." A sound piece of advice except for the NAR part, since the Northern Alberta Railway was always late for everything, but Josephine got the message. Advice about abstinence was often accompanied with a lot of talk about "pure thoughts." If pure thoughts didn't work, one doctor had this advice for a patient who'd already had more babies than she could handle: "Tell Jake to sleep on the roof."

The Safe Period? Oh, You Gambler!

Georgina Sackville in Calgary tried to help women prevent conception, but she came armed with words only. Her chief concern was for unmarried women who "were betrayed into relinquishing their virtue by the lying promises of young men who disappeared" as soon as pregnancy was discovered.

> 'Twas the same old wretched story that for ages bards have sung,
> 'Twas a woman weak and wanton and a villain's tempting tongue.

That's how Sackville began one of the publications she wrote during the 1930s. It was called *Birth Control: The Prevention of Conception.* This would have led the women who paid their one dollar for it to think they might actually learn how to stop having babies. But there are so many words, so many Bible verses, and so much Christian moralizing that it's very hard to find actual advice on birth control. Sackville

couldn't exactly draw pictures, of course, because it was still illegal to talk about birth control. She had to bury her advice deep in turns of phrase such as: "Through you and your child the rivulet of life will flow on through endless time." Does that sound like birth control to you?

But Sackville writes very cleverly. Without offending the prevailing moral code, she manages to suggest that women do have some power in the marriage equation and that they might actually use that power. And she does get to birth control eventually, but it's the old rhythm or safe-period advice. First, she cites sev-

The year 1911 was big for the birth of babies in Didsbury, Alberta. Some of the new mothers lined up for a picture to document their achievements. Fashions are still Edwardian, especially the hats.
(COURTESY GLENBOW ARCHIVES)

eral eminent British doctors. Then she takes a very long time to explain the process of menstruation. If you're still with her, she finally steps up to the plate:

> There are but two periods in a healthy human female when normal pregnancy cannot take place. These times are three or four days before the menstrual period and again from one to ten days after the cessation of the menstrual discharge.

She came close. Doctors now know that ovulation happens mid-cycle. To be more specific, if the first day of the period is day one, ovulation happens around day sixteen, give or take a day or two, and that's when intercourse should be avoided. It was still problematic science, but Sackville was on the right track. Her system worked nine times out of ten, she claimed, and it was certainly better than nothing, which is what the world offered women in those days as far as birth control was concerned. Also, her mathematics didn't offend the church or break the law.

It might also be a good idea to skip the sex act now and then, she said, because science has shown that less frequent intercourse enhances ecstasy. "Suppose New Year came once a week, we should take less pleasure in fifty-two New Years than we do in one now because frequency would render it insipid," she argued. However, she did throw a bone to those who didn't find sex insipid, no matter how often, when she said that less frequent intercourse can double, perhaps even quadruple, all the endowments of the offspring.

It's easy to make fun of all these grand words and noble intentions, but it's not really fair. Sackville didn't write this from on high. She was no lady bountiful telling the peasants how to live. She ran a shelter for children of unwed mothers, counseled and helped many unfortunate women and in the end wrote this dangerous piece about birth control. She had to have it vetted by a lawyer and approved by several church leaders in the city, but she published it, bless her. At least it spoke directly the words "birth control"—two of the most dangerous words in the English language in the bad old days.

She's Havin' My Baby

Paul Anka may have thought that havin' a baby was fun and a great tribute to manhood generally, but women didn't always see it that way. In the early days, it was a scary business, a gamble. Some women got through it easily, others suffered fiercely and some died. That was the prospect pregnant women faced. Will I be able to do it? Will I be alone? Will I die? Yes, no and maybe.

Even when anesthetics such as chloroform came along, there was debate as to whether they should be used during childbirth since they might "interfere with the consequences of Eve's transgression." That mean-spirited idea relates to the Biblical story of Eve, who apparently let sin into the world by eating the apple in the Garden of Eden. By so doing, she and all her descendants would be sentenced to painful childbirth for ever and ever, which somehow made it all right that women weren't given much help in childbirth.

One of the drugs used in the 1930s and 1940s was called "twilight sleep," a mixture of scopolamine and morphine. It was supposed to relieve the pain, but some women reacted so negatively that they had to be restrained so they wouldn't come to harm. In the case of Margaret S., the doctor bound her wrists to the delivery table, but she was in such a state that she broke the restraints. How she and the baby survived is a wonder. Mrs. S. talked about that twilight sleep for the rest of her life.

Childbirth is the one female experience that women do talk about, though not the private parts of it, of course. The words of birth and the physical parts involved remain unmentionable, but the parts about getting the doctor and being in labor for two days and breaking the restraints—all those things turn up in local history books. It's the one measure of a woman's courage that can be mentioned, even boasted about. They suffered such pain and fear with so little to comfort them medically or emotionally. No wonder they mentioned it now and then.

But not every woman survived to tell her story. If she didn't, there's just the sentence in the local history book that John Brown's first wife died in childbirth. And then we're told he got himself another wife. That was the brutal truth. If a woman died in childbirth, another woman had to be found.

Childbirth was often a figure-it-out-for-yourself problem. If you were lucky, there was a hospital nearby or a doctor who would hitch up horse and buggy to come for the delivery. If that wasn't possible, a woman could hope to get an aboriginal woman to help. These women had looked after birthing for thousands of years, so they were good at it. That's what happened for Sarah Brick, whose children were all born in

Fort Vermilion before doctors, hospitals and airplanes.

Sometimes a female relative would come for a long visit to be present at the birth and help afterward. Most often she would be a spinster aunt or sister who was able to go where needed for births, illnesses and deaths. These were the informal systems that existed for health care—nothing as dependable and scientific as exists now, but the best systems under the circumstances.

Even a city hospital and a lot of money didn't guarantee anything. Georgina Hope Hespeler married Augustus Nanton in Winnipeg in 1886. It was a union of two of Winnipeg's richest families. But Georgina died a year later in childbirth. The cause of her death was quite likely childbed fever brought on by the doctor who likely didn't wash his hands and equipment between deliveries. Three other new mothers died the same week, all patients of the same doctor. There were no antibiotics then. If you got an infection, you died.

Some women nevertheless seemed to be invincible and delivered their babies easily. Dr. Mary Percy Jackson moved from England to northern Alberta in 1929 because she thought it would be a grand adventure. It was. A few months after her arrival, she attended a maternity

case and found the baby born, washed, and the new mother down on her hands and knees scrubbing the floor. The woman spoke no English, but Dr. Jackson explained by various signs that she ought to go to bed and take it easy for a while. "And when I told her husband she should go to bed for seven days, he translated to her and they both roared with laughter." You have to love the strength, even as you wonder whether the baby made it. Jackson also mentioned in her account of this birth that she expected they had "some food somewhere but I didn't see any signs."

Wherever and however the births happened, it was still the age-old story: a new life, a miracle. Kate Brighty Colley was a public health nurse in the Edmonton area when she was called out one day to help an aboriginal woman in childbirth. She encountered conditions quite different from anything she'd been trained for. The mother-to-be was not on a bed. She was squatting and hanging onto the tent pole, a dirt floor beneath her. Her toddler son was trotting in and out of the tent. Nothing was sterile, in the hospital sense of the term, but when the baby was born, he was fine. His big brother howled, the father beat a hasty retreat, but the baby was there, a new little person. "For aught we knew the sun, moon and planets might all have stood still, for there in that rough tent had been witnessed the greatest and oldest drama known to man, the birth of a new being," she wrote later in her book *While Rivers Flow.*

Whither Thou Goest

Marie-Anne Lagemodière (née Gaboury) was a great role model. She started the 1800s in grand style by saying to her husband, "No, I'm not going to stay at home. I'm coming with you." Jean-Baptiste, a free trader with fur companies, hadn't counted on that. When he had married her in April 1806, he had promised that he wouldn't go back to his old voyageur life. He would stay home in Quebec and be a good farmer.

But when the ice broke up in the St. Lawrence that spring, he couldn't resist the call of the wild. He had to go west to wheel and deal in furs, to get occasional work with the fur traders, to live life on the edge. It was in his blood, he pleaded to his wife. "Just let me go and I'll be back in a year or two."

She didn't believe him and started packing. So Marie-Anne became a contender for the title of First White Woman in the West. Perhaps she was, perhaps she wasn't. There's also the story of Isobel Gunn, an Orkney woman, who pretended to be a man and was hired by the Hudson's Bay Company. One day in December 1806, while working at the Pembina trading post, she felt unwell—and gave birth to a baby. Once the truth was out, she was shipped back to Scotland and lived unhappily ever after. Even had the father of her child come to her rescue—though there's no hint that he did—she would not have been allowed to stay. Fur-trading employees could not bring wives from away.

Marie-Anne's husband, however, was a free trader. He could take as many wives or companions as he wanted. That's why she accompanied him as far as Pembina the first summer—she who had never been farther than a few miles from her village. She learned many things on that first trip. How to sit completely still in a canoe for hours on end. How to stumble through rock and bush on the numerous portages. How to make camp and feed Jean-Baptiste. How to sleep in a tent through mosquitoes thick and thin. How to manage her female body without any fuss. She was pregnant by the time they set out on this hair-raising trip, so she didn't have to worry about menstrual periods, but she did have to wonder about the birth of her first child. As usual, she managed. Her daughter Reine

L2383—**Chambers, Premier Ware.**

No. 20.	30c
No. 22.	35c
No. 24.	45c

L2384—**Chambers, Granite Ware.**

No. 20.	27c
No. 22.	30c
No. 24.	35c

L2385—Cuspidors, Premier Ware, 8½ inch, 55c; Club pattern..................... 65c
L2386—Cuspidors, Granite Ware.......... 15c
L2387—Cuspidors, Premier Ware.......... 17c

L2388—Chamber Pails, galvanized, 12 qt........ 50c
16 qt.............. 60c

L2389—Chamber Pails, granite ware, 14 qt........ $1.00

L2390—Commode, Premier Ware.............. $2.50

L2391—Child's Bath, Japanned oak, 26 in... $1.10
30 inch, $1.35; 36 inch................. 1.65

L2392—Bed Pan, gray granite, as cut....... $1.25
L2393—Bed Pan, square................. 1.00

Most chamber pots were no-nonsense granite containers that were hidden under the bed. Their existence might have remained secret but for the fact that they were noisy to use. (HUDSON'S BAY CATALOGUE, 1910)

was born at the Hudson's Bay Company fort in Pembina in January 1807. A few months later, Reine was laced into an Indian cradle, attached to her mother's saddle, and off they headed farther west toward Edmonton. How did Marie-Anne manage her personal needs and those of a baby who needed changing? There were no diapers, no drugstores along the way. There were aboriginal women, however, and they may have demonstrated the use of moss for various human needs. Marie-Anne, of course, never mentions any of this.

Marie-Anne had her second baby in the middle of a buffalo hunt on the prairie. She named him fittingly La Prairie, but it was later officially changed to Jean-Baptiste. Her third baby came long when they were camping near the Cypress Hills. She was named Cyprès by her mother, but that lovely name was also changed. There were five more children. The second to last was a girl they named Julie, who became the mother of Louis Riel.

The Little House of Many Names

The outhouse, the little house, the back house and the white house. The privy, the biffy, the loo and the library. In its grander moments, it was called the house of lords, the ladies' chamber, and the throne. In its humbler moments, it was known as the shack out back, the comfort station, the restroom and the john.

It had more names than any other building, but the names were seldom used. It was, of course, the outdoor toilet, and it was invisible as far as polite society was concerned.

The silence and secrecy surrounding the outhouse made life doubly difficult for women. Because of the complications of menstruation, they had to use these unmentionable places more often than men, but they had to keep everything private. A woman couldn't say right out to her husband, "I'm going to the john. You finish canning the fifty quarts of berries I just picked." No, she had to finish the canning, make sure the baby was safe, rush off to the john, wrestle the door shut since nobody else bothered to close it, complete her task, then pick up a log or two for the wood box on the way back and pretend she'd been out for a breath of fresh air. Outhouses were often deliberately located so that the woman of the house had to pass the clothesline, the garden and the woodpile, the better to pick up one or more items on her way back to disguise the reason for her absence.

For Esme Tuck, it was a pleasure trip in summer, with pansies planted along the path and squirrels and chipmunks "with a charming lack of modesty" visiting her in the biffy overlooking the Pouce Coupe River. But in winter, her "house of necessity" became a house of torture. "I would charge headlong through the snow, clutching a hot water bottle under my parka, one big protest against inexorable nature," she wrote of those winter trips. "One was assaulted above and below," she wrote in her *Peace River Chronicles.*

Before indoor plumbing, the chamber pot was the other option for women. Of course it was not mentioned in polite company either, unless it went by some other name such as thunder mug, lollipop pail or commode. The commode was actually the piece of furniture in which the humble pot, by whatever name, resided. But not everybody could afford a piece of furniture to hold the pot, so the word commode was downsized to mean just the pot itself. And without furniture to hold it and hide it, it was generally to be found under the bed.

Most chamber pots were rather plain, at least in the earliest days of settlement. Who had the space or money for a crockery pot with decorated handles and a lid? A plain white or blue enamel container did the job. Then, since a woman couldn't admit to bodily parts and functions, she had to figure out how to use the pot without making a noise, for the enamel pot wasn't called a thunder mug for nothing.

"The proper use of a chamber pot is an art in itself," one woman described. "First you must ascertain whether you have an enamel or china pot. The enamel is very noisy; any self-respecting user would put it on the end of the bed while using it and thus muffle the sound," she continued. "If it had a lid, the proper procedure was to take a newspaper and lay it over the pot before putting the lid on. This of course was again to muffle the sound of a lid banging."

Then the user had to figure out how to empty the thing without anyone noticing—as if she were the only person among them who had to relieve her bladder. It was all very curious, this need to keep all bathroom functions under wraps. And this embarrassment and modesty was passed on to future generations of girls who, as soon as they were old enough, had to take on the pot-emptying chores for the family.

School outhouses were no picnic either. Some were a double arrangement: boys on one side of a wooden partition, girls on the other. Girls could

never go if a boy was in the vicinity. He might hear her, or a whole gang of them might surround the building and throw rocks. This was the height of embarrassment and another reason for girls to learn iron control.

In a one-room schoolhouse in Manitoba, the toilet seat was kept hanging out in the open on the wall of the classroom, the better to keep it warm. When students had to go, they picked up the seat, lugged it out to the biffy and used it there. Then they'd bring the seat back and hang it once more on the wall. A sensible idea.

Rest rooms were a sensible idea too. The term *rest room* is not, however, a synonym for bathroom, though there may have been an outdoor biffy nearby or a proper bathroom in the building. Rest rooms in western Canada between 1910 and 1950 or thereabouts were several rooms or a house established in small towns so that a woman from out of town had somewhere to wait for her husband, a place to change the baby or feed it, or perhaps to make a cup of tea. These places of refuge were all over the West. Alberta had forty-eight in 1922, Manitoba had more than sixty through the years, but most shut down after World War II. While they lasted, however, they were a real western phenomenon, the forerunner of social services.

The rooms were usually the project of a local branch of the Women's Institute (WI), whose members raised money for their rest rooms in a lovely variety of ways. In Cereal, Alberta, WI members raised funds by sewing shirts and selling them to the bachelors of the community. In McLennan, Alberta, members made a "Grandmother's Garden" quilt from weekly patterns appearing in the *Edmonton Journal* throughout 1928 and then raffled it. Chicken suppers, rummage sales, tag days were other ways of raising money in days gone by to keep the rest rooms open for the benefit of rural women.

After all, a woman wasn't allowed into the local bar, where her husband may have been. The town may not have had a library so she couldn't wait there, and she couldn't just knock on someone's door and ask if she could come in. But she could go to the rest room, where, with any luck, she'd be able to put her feet up and talk to another woman. Finding female company was not the easiest thing to do in the early part of the century, considering distances and modes of transportation. So rest rooms did double duty as a place of shelter when needed and as a place to find the company of other women.

What Did You Do in the War, Mommy?

When Great Britain declared war on Germany in 1914—the start of the Great War that was supposed to end all wars—Canada declared war too. We were a British colony, after all, so we sent men first, then horses, troops, equipment, food and nurses. And socks. Canadian women picked up knitting needles in 1914 and didn't set them down until the end of the war in 1918.

Even schoolgirls were expected to knit. Eula Carscallen of Red Deer recorded in her diary that there was one knitting period a week at school in 1918, "and we were all making amputation socks."

Private Timothy Kelly from Lethbridge arrived in France on September 5, wrote one letter home and died in battle on September 30. His wife then did what women do. She grieved for her husband, then got to work and looked after their six children. Other women grieved for sons and fathers. Then they too did what had to be done in their own private wars.

It wasn't just men who went overseas. As Marjorie Barron records in her history of wartime nursing, when Mary Florence Rodd left Calgary in 1915 to serve with the Canadian Army Medical

Corps nursing service, she told the local newspaper:

> I know it is going to be hard work all the time, but that is what I want. I simply want to know and feel I am doing something for the country. Oh, yes, it will be an ordeal all right but it must be worse of an ordeal for the brave boys who will be wounded. I must say I am glad to be going and I am prepared to stay until it is all over.

A total of 2,504 Canadian women served as nurses in Europe during the four years of battle, and 46 died over there.

Thanks to the war that didn't end all wars, women finally got a chance to work outside the home at jobs normally done by men. Women in eastern Canada moved into factory jobs in munitions plants. Western women hitched up the plow and kept the farm going, or they got office or clerking jobs in banks and stores. Between 1911 and 1921, the number of women in clerical jobs in the West doubled, inspiring such dubious reactions as the poem, "Girls in the Office," in the *Lethbridge Herald* in 1916.

The office is really now a different place
For every man works with a smile on

The Kelly family from Lethbridge, Alberta, posed for this photo in 1916 just before Private Timothy Kelly left for France as part of the 31st Battalion of the Canadian Expeditionary Force. Kelly is forty-seven, past the compulsory age for enlistment, he has six children, but he's going anyway. That decision changed everything for his family. (COURTESY KEVIN MACLEAN, LETHBRIDGE)

his face
It's certainly evident such is the case
Because we've got girls in the office.
The office boy formerly looked such a
    wreck
Now with clean collars, his form he'll
    bedeck
Indeed, it is whispered, he washes his
    neck
Now we've got girls in the office.
We "Mister" each other formally now
And never by chance kick up a row
Our conduct's exemplary, all must allow
Since we've got girls in the office.

A later line in the poem mentions that powder's been seen on the manager's sleeve, which would never do in our politically correct age, but obviously the female workers were making a difference. It was such a liberating experience for many women that they didn't want to give up their jobs at the end of the war. But being the good sports, they relinquished the jobs to the men who returned, didn't complain too much and carried on.

Mrs. J.A. Massey of High River, Alberta, deserves a medal for wartime contributions. As recorded in the local history, *The Roaring Twenties*, she made 5,545 buttonholes in a variety of garments for war effort, and she made every one of those buttonholes from scratch, by hand, with needle and thread. From March 1915 to January 1919, Mrs. Massey also knitted or sewed 3,567 articles for the Red Cross, turning out an average of 2.5 articles a day. Altogether, she used 661 spools of thread, a lot of which went into those thousands of buttonholes. The list of her war-time accomplishments is remarkable:

- 620 day shirts
- 389 suits of pajamas
- 236 bandages
- 453 khaki slings
- 318 pillow covers
- 259 kit and property bags
- 151 bath robes and dressing gowns
- 272 stretcher caps
- 188 amputation covers
- 156 McNaughton bandages
- 7 knitted eye bandages
- 84 water bottle covers
- 6 nurse aprons
- 8 nightshirts
- 14 towels
- 204 handkerchiefs
- 12 ward slippers
- 6 bed socks
- 129 pairs of knitted socks
- 18 knitted sock feet

The very first advertisement for Kotex sanitary pads. It's a marvel of advertising in that it doesn't mention what is being advertised other than to say it's a "woman's article." The picture accompanying this careful prose is a painting of a group of people: a veteran in a wheelchair to remind everyone about the valiant fighting men; a nurse; and a woman who is obviously the man's loving and faithful wife. A younger woman, perhaps the daughter of the veteran, rests under a nearby tree that shelters them all, just as Kotex will shelter them all. It is a masterful combination of symbols that never once gets into embarrassing territory. The ad appeared in women's magazines in January 1921.

(COURTESY KIMBERLY-CLARK)

Just as every item on this list represents a woman who cared deeply about the men and women fighting a war for peace and goodness, so every item also represents something awful: amputated limbs, feet rotted in cold, wet trenches, wounds of all description on men far from home and comfort.

Kotex—Thanks to War and Nurses

Up to the end of the First World War, women could buy disposable sanitary pads from the catalogue, but they were relatively expensive. Most women made their own from flannel material, devised their own harnesses to keep the pads in place, and generally made the best of a bad situation. The only thing that commerce offered in the way of assistance was a rubber apron that wrapped from back · to front to help keep stains off clothing. It was like wearing a rubber diaper, and made the whole process even more uncomfortable. And the flannel always had to be washed, of course.

Then, one day, nurses overseas realized that certain bandages looked about the right size for a menstrual pad. It was one of those Eureka moments. The disposable sanitary pad was born. Well, not quite that quickly. When the war ended in 1918, the bandage manufacturer, Cellucotton, realized they'd have to find another market for their products. They tiptoed into the market with Kotex.

Making the pads was easy. They'd been making bandages all along. But how do you let the world know that you have this new product for menstrual periods? People wouldn't even say the words. The deafening silence out there made it a big risk for Cellucotton, so they began a series of very careful advertisements.

In January 1921 the very first ad for Kotex proclaimed:

New but tried and proved, Kotex enters universal service from a romantic background. For, although a woman's article, it started as Cellucotton, a wonderful sanitary absorbent which science perfected for use of our men and allied soldiers wounded in France. With peace came an idea suggested in letters from nurses regarding a new use for this wonderful absorbent, and early in 1919 our laboratory made the first sanitary pads of Cellucotton enclosed in gauze and placed them on sale in various cities. Requests for more followed every sale, and we devoted two years to perfecting the new article—named KOTEX from "cotton-like texture"—and to the

Kotex, the product that could not be mentioned, was nevertheless advertised widely. In this April 1928 advertisement in Chatelaine *magazine, the emphasis is on a doctor's advice. The "doctor," however, still doesn't use any unmentionable words.* (COURTESY KIMBERLY-CLARK)

Are you in the know?

How to brighten these blinkers?
☐ *Read the funny papers*
☐ *Mooch Mom's mascara*
☐ *Quick, Watson—the eye pads*

Dreary-eyed? When you want to be starry-eyed? Just rest your lids beneath a pair of moist eye pads. Jiffy-quick, their soothing liquid eases the ache—brings back the twinkle to tired optics. Comfort and "sparkle" are first cousins. That's why, on certain days, so many bright young chicks insist on Kotex sanitary napkins. For Kotex has *dependable* softness. Unlike pads that just "feel" soft at first touch, Kotex is made to *stay soft while wearing*. Free from bunching, roping, you're far more comfortable with Kotex.

If you loathe setting-up exercises, try—
☐ *The Lazy Mae routine*
☐ *A starvation diet*
☐ *A new girdle*

For setting-up without getting up—try the Lazy Mae routine! Prone in bed, stretch for your tootsies ten times. Bicycle your legs two minutes, then pull them back till toes contact bed headboard. Keeping trim props up your poise. On problem days, Kotex bolsters your confidence—with the plus protection of that special *safety centre*. Only Kotex gives you this *plus* protection—with the patented 4-ply safety centre you can be sure of avoiding accidental! That's why problem days aren't problems . . . when you choose Kotex!

When he says "I've enjoyed meeting you"—should you say ☐ *"Thank you"*
☐ *"Same to you"*
☐ *"Likewise"*

You may feel that the pleasure is all yours—but only a goobrain would say so. A gracious "thank you" suffices. (Your tone can tell him it's mutual.) Reserve is becoming. Keep a secret or two. There's one secret that's tattle-proof—when you trust to Kotex on trying days. Because only Kotex has patented, *flat tapered ends* that don't show. Strictly out of this world compared to thick, stubby pads, Kotex's flat pressed ends don't cause revealing outlines. So . . . with Kotex, no one will know.

More women choose KOTEX* than all other sanitary napkins put together

By 1945, Kotex had begun its popular "Are You In The Know?" series in which questions were supposedly posed to women, mostly young women, and the answers always came around to Kotex. In between was advice about deportment, dress, behavior, and dating habits — Kotex was influencing more than just the management of menstruation.
(COURTESY KIMBERLY-CLARK)

building of machinery which makes and seals it hygienically without contact of human hands. Kotex are now ready for every woman's use.

But they're actually selling you sanitary pads. You'll buy them if you can afford them, and you'll be glad. When Kotex cottoned on to the fact that women were embarrassed to ask for the plain blue Kotex box, they suggested to their dealers that they set up a small box beside the cash register. Women could then deposit their money, pick up a box (wrapped in plain brown paper, as if that fooled anyone), and melt away into the background before anyone realized they're buying (gasp) a box of Kotex.

By July 1921, the Kotex ads featured a woman in evening dress sashaying down a curved staircase, flowers surrounding her. This image, again a painting, was clearly intended for those who could afford Kotex. The next ad tried to appeal to both ends of the financial spectrum. Headed "Simplify the laundress problem," it featured two women, one the lady of the house, the other the laundress. The laundress looked bedraggled, apparently tired from washing all the menstrual paraphernalia of her employer. Thus, Kotex aimed to liberate both the washerwoman and her mistress.

The first Kotex magazine advertisement to feature a photograph of a woman created quite a stir in 1928. The public could apparently take ads for sanitary pads as long as the illustrations were stylized. But to show a real woman? No! There were letters of protest to the magazines in question, quiet chats among the members of the Ladies Aid, generalized remarks from the pulpit about the place of women and modesty and so on. Today it's hard to believe all that fuss.

Even the woman pictured in the advertisement was upset that her photo was being used in such a way. It was true, she said, that she had posed for a photographer and had signed a release, but she did not appreciate ending up promoting Kotex. She was mortified.

This problem of mortification continued for many years. In Grimshaw, Alberta, in 1950, when a main-street fire was dynamited to put it out, some windows in town were blown out. It was midwinter. Cold air poured into the open buildings. So the druggist came to the rescue with a few big empty cardboard boxes. Opened up, they made excellent coverings for the windows. But next morning when the smoke cleared, the residents discovered that the cardboard over their windows stated, in bold blue letters for everyone to see, KOTEX. "Well, now it is something to laugh about, but in those days it was a 'no-know,'" Irene McFaddin wrote years later in *Land of Hope and Dreams.* Many women were clearly using Kotex since the local druggist had lots of boxes. All the same, the name shocked the town.

Cheaper by the Dozen

Frank and Lillian Gilbreth, husband and wife, were time and efficiency experts who applied some of their theories to raising their twelve children, an experiment that resulted in the book *Cheaper by the Dozen.* Written by several of the children, the book was a great hit and became a movie by the same name. Today, the Gilbreths seem more like fiction than fact, but they really did have twelve children, and they really did walk the walk of their efficiency theories.

Dr. Lillian Gilbreth was hired in 1927 by Johnson & Johnson. This company also manufactured sanitary products—eventually called Modess—but in 1927 it was losing out to the makers of Kotex. They hired Gilbreth to find out what women liked and disliked about menstrual products. No one had thought to ask women before. Gilbreth sent out questionnaires, talked to women and came up with these very modern suggestions:

> It is essential that a woman be added to the staff of Johnson & Johnson and that all products be submitted to women for inspection of design and tests for actual use. No laboratory devices for testing can take the place of actual wear. The product must be tested by various types of women who make maximum demands of some sort.

She then added that a campaign should be undertaken to address the fact "that the normal woman (during her menstrual period) can safely pursue her usual program and profit by so doing." In other words, stop suggesting that menstruation is a debilitating condition. It's just part of being a woman.

Whether Modess took her advice or not, Kotex certainly did. In the *Canadian Home Journal*, October 1936, a half-page advertisement appeared with the headline "Women Ask Me: 'What does Kotex Offer that Others Don't?'" The answers were supplied by Mary Pauline Callender, described as an authority on feminine hygiene. As Gilbreth had recommended, a woman answered the question, and she used words that women could identify with. "Kotex can't chafe, Kotex can't fail, Kotex can't show." Just what women wanted to hear. Kotex was obviously winning the war of sanitary napkins at this stage. The accompanying pictures showed women playing basketball, riding bikes and preparing to go out for an evening in a clingy, flowing dress that would certainly betray any lumps and bumps.

Other issues of the *Canadian Home Journal* in the 1930s also featured half-page ads for Kotex, masterfully written and illustrated, with no mention of "menstruation" or "blood" or "crotch" or any other word that might associate Kotex with any of those unmentionables. It's a product that gives peace of mind, soft protection, delightful freedom. They are remarkable advertisements that successfully marketed a product, the purpose of which could not be mentioned.

Chapter 4
Washing and Warming the West

★　　　★　　　★　　　★　　　★

WOMEN IN THE EARLY DAYS CLEANED, washed, swept, scrubbed, planted. They made the place look better, and they made the people around them feel better. That work by women may not be as unmentionable as corsets, birth control, and menstruation, but it certainly was not mentioned. It was a given. That's what women did and that's all there was to it, but it made all the difference. Single men couldn't wait to find themselves wives, even if they had to come via mail order. Married men couldn't wait to bring their wives from the Ukraine or England or China to help them survive in this new country, to make a home and a life. It's not the stuff of headlines, but it should at least be mentioned, acknowledged, even saluted. So many women I talked to said something like, "Oh, I never did anything important." I could have cried. Even they don't mention and take credit for the important and difficult work they did.

Take the matter of laundry. It was an horrendous task before the advent of electricity and running water. Think again of the Saskatchewan farmer's wife who wrote to the prime minister for new underwear for her husband. It was a wonderful coup that he sent it, but then what? She was the one who had to wash it along with all the other dirty clothes, a process that would take her the better part of a day and probably the next day to get the clean clothes dry and do the ironing. Did her work make the history books? Occasionally, but not often. As Mrs. Heinz

Exner explained in the local history book *Mosquitoes, Muskeg and Memories,*

> There are elements of my past that I do not long for. Laundry for example. No, I never washed clothes with a tub and washboard. But that old wringer washer sent shivers down my spine whenever someone's undies went around and around the rollers instead of squishing neatly between them as the manufacturer had intended. But worse was winter laundry. Etched in my mind is a picture of my father's long underwear (these also had a trap door) having been washed and rinsed, hung on the clothesline to "dry" in the dead of winter, then carried back to the house, stiffly frozen, and laid out on the kitchen table to thaw.

She doesn't tell us how long the underwear dripped on a line in the house before finally dried. It would have taken days, which proves there's more than one way to define unmentionable. What about diapers? Pampers weren't available until 1961. Until then, it was cloth diapers on wash day, not to mention sore, red hands for the washerwoman. Those are key words—"Not to mention." So much of women's work was not mentioned.

Bugs and vermin were another silent battle fought by women. If they succeeded, their family had status. If not, less status. My mother, for instance, discovered on her wedding night in 1935 that her new husband's homestead house was buggy. They had been married in Peace River in the afternoon, then went home to the house that evening, where a group of neighbors was waiting to charivari them—that is, to welcome them, hoot and holler a bit, and have some lunch. In the course of the festivities, my mother heard some of the guests mentioning that the mosquitoes were sure bad that night. It was then she realized that the mosquitoes weren't bad at all. Something else must be at work. And indeed they were, but they were bedbugs. She spent the next few weeks pouring boiling water into the cracks of the log house, putting the bed legs into a vile solution called creoline so the bugs wouldn't climb into their bed, and moving out dirty clothes and bedding. She washed and aired and cleaned so thoroughly that she won the battle temporarily, enough so that she could hold up her head in the community, but there was always a chance the bugs would move in again. Constant vigilance was necessary.

Catalogues helped with the bug battles since they were also the equivalent of drugstores for rural folk. You want mouse traps, flea powder, fly catchers? Send away to Eaton's or any one of the catalogue companies that served rural areas. And while you're leafing through the catalogue, check out the styles. Are dresses longer this year? Sleeves fuller? And how would rayon panties feel after so many years of wearing fleece bloomers? Thus were catalogues the most practical book in the house but also dream books. Sometimes, the only books in fact.

Of course, that's where the men of the family got their underwear as well. Their long johns.

Stanfield's was such a well-known Canadian institution that it was even mentioned in at least one Christmas pageant according to Pat McDonald's *Where the River Brought Them*. Young Robert was the narrator for the local Christmas program in Rocky Mountain House in the 1930s. He had his lines down pat except that he couldn't remember the name *Nazareth*, so his mother took an indelible pencil and wrote the elusive word on the top inside his woolen underwear. All he had to do, she assured him, was check the back of his underwear if he got stuck.

It's washing day on the prairies. You can't see the men's underwear on the clothesline yet, but they'll be there in all their glory, ready to freeze stiff as a board, then be brought in to finish drying inside the house. (COURTESY PROVINCIAL ARCHIVES OF ALBERTA)

STANFIELD'S
"It wears longer" *Unshrinkable*
UNDERWEAR

STANFIELD'S is cut to fit perfectly. Made of the best grade wool, it is warm, comfortable and durable, does not bind the shoulders, and will not shrink. All good dealers sell Stanfield's.

Made in Combinations and Two-piece suits, in full length, knee and elbow length, and sleeveless. Stanfield's Adjustable Combinations and Sleepers for growing children. (Patented).

For sample book showing weights and textures, write

**Stanfield's Limited
Truro, N. S.** 35

"Stands Strenuous Wear"

An underwear ad in a Canadian catalogue also hints at the scientific and medical benefits of wool. They're a product of Canada's own underwear specialist, Stanfield's of Nova Scotia. (CANADIAN HOME JOURNAL, NOVEMBER 1920)

(You can see this coming.) All was calm, all was bright until Robert did indeed forget the name. So he tugged at his underwear, saw the name and said in a strong confident voice, "From Stanfield's came Mary and Joseph weary, but no one would take them in."

The Trap Door:
Perhaps a Canadian First

In the early days, long underwear for men came in two pieces: a shirt and long drawers of wool or cotton, the drawers held up around the waist with drawstrings or with elastic when it became available. The style left a lot of bulk around the middle. Then along came one-piece long underwear known as combinations, and most men switched. Combinations were warmer, neater and handier. The only problem was the back door. Some of the earlier versions, known as "open crotch" underwear, had a vertical opening at the back with flaps of material that could be parted, then folded back together again. It made for a tidier waistline, but it meant a lumpy back end because it was difficult to fold the two flaps neatly together into a smooth line. Men complained that it was a "humpy, lumpy, creasy, baggy proposition that chafed your nethers."

That's when a small woolen mill in

Truro, Nova Scotia, came up with what they called a drop-seat style and began selling "closed crotch" underwear. It was such a simple solution—a single piece of fabric that could be unbuttoned, folded down, then buttoned up again—that men soon preferred it to the older version. Thus was born the trap door of legend and song.

Charles Stanfield came to Canada from England in 1855 and established his mill in Truro in 1870. A creative genius, he was always experimenting with new ideas and machines for knitted products and turned out underwear, sweaters and stockings. By the time he retired in 1896 and his sons took over the business, he had already designed and sold a version of the drop-seat underwear. However, he didn't patent the design. So when a Canadian-born mill worker in the United States came up with what he called the "Kenosha Klosed Krotch Underwear" in 1909, his company—now the Jockey Company— immediately patented it as their own. Still, judging by the dates, this all-important piece of underwear history seems to have been a Canadian first.

Over the years, Stanfield's and other mills learned how to shrink-proof underwear fabric. This was a great boon for women who up till then had not only had to wash the underwear but also shape it after washing, stretching it so it would fit again. Maybe that's why women didn't object too much when their men wore one pair of underwear for months at a time. Drying wet woolen underwear in winter was also problematic. If it was hung inside, people had to duck dripping underwear legs dangling from a clothesline in the house. If it was hung outside, it froze stiff as a board, and still had to be hung inside later. The care and maintenance of long underwear in winter was no laughing matter although it had its moments. Dawn Stephenson remembers bringing in her dad's underwear in the frozen state and then waltzing with it until it slowly warmed up and collapsed in her arms. It was the only enjoyable part of the whole process, she said.

In the 1920s underwear manufacturers began to use bleach that didn't smell like sulfur, another boon for the wearer and the woman who slept beside him every night. They also came up with a process to remove the sticks and burrs in natural wool, which took away some of the itch. From then on, the manufacture of underwear gradually improved—better fabrics, elastic, buttons and styling—until the garments didn't look like underwear at all. All that remained were the legends.

Even with the advent of electric washing machines, washdays were still blue when I had to hang clothes on the line, fingers so frozen they felt like they would snap off. A few hours later, I dragged those same clothes, now stiff and unwieldy, back into the house to hang them over the line strung across the kitchen. An old wooden clothes horse creaked and groaned under the weight of the extras. A trip across the room meant ducking to avoid being slapped in the face with the frozen underwear legs. The house was as cold as the outside until they thawed out and dried.
—Jean Fahlman, "Washday Blues."

Underwear.

Men's Heavy All-Wool Shirts and Drawers—
50c. each.

Special value in Non-shrinkable All-Wool-Shirts and Drawers, at 65c. and 69c. each, in grey, flesh and blue-grey.

The following are Scotch Lamb's Wool Non-shrinkable Shirts and Drawers, hand knitted and well finished, with double or single breast in shirts.

	S. Men's.	Men's.	O.S. Men's.
12 Gage	$2.50.		
14 "	$3.25.	$3.25.	$3.75.
18 "	$4.00.	$4.00.	$4.75.

Heavy Union Underwear—
70, 80 and 90c. per suit, full sizes.

Boys' sizes in heavy, plain and ribbed Union Shirts and Drawers—
From 50c. to $1.00 per suit, and in All-Wool at 50, 60, 65 and 75c. each.

Men's Heavy Unbleached Cotton Underwear—
50, 60, 70 and 90c. per suit.

Men's Merino Underwear—
75c. per suit; sizes 34 to 40 inches.

Men's underwear advertised in Eaton's catalogue, Fall and Winter 1889. No pictures, just description.

May 24 was the accepted day for the changing of the guard—long underwear off, summer underwear on. And even if it was cold that day, the change was made with pleasure. In *The Spirit of Ghost Pine*, Henry Kaatiala describes what he wore to school through the winter months:

I rode a horse to the Turtle School, two and a half miles away. In the winter, I had to wear long johns, wool stockings and black felt boots which always made my feet so itchy, and so many other clothes it was a wonder I could move, much less get on a horse. The school was always cold so we had to be dressed for that too.

For the youngsters who were sewn into their underwear in November, the May 24 switch was like losing a second skin. For those who sat next to them at school or church, that change of underwear must have been like a breath of fresh air.

John J. Molgat, who grew up in Ste. Rose Du Lac, Manitoba, remembered the first day of donning long underwear in the fall, the ritual that confirmed the onset of winter:

Although I have not worn them since that time, I still have fond memories of the 'day of the changeover,' the feeling of soft cuddly warmth from ankles to neck as the combination wrapped itself around you. Being the oldest in the family had many drawbacks: I was forever cautioned to 'set a good example for my little brothers' or urged to allow them this or that privilege 'because they are smaller than you are.' The Day of the Fleece Underwear brought compensation because if the smallest brother had outgrown the hand-me-down from the previous year, these were discarded and all sizes shifted down one, leaving a vacancy at the top and I, the eldest, received a brand-new set with fleece of maximum fuzziness.

Underwear and its trap door were the butt of many jokes and stories. One story concerns a husband and wife who were traveling by horse and buggy when night overtook them. They stopped at a house along the road that belonged to a bachelor who made them welcome. He shared a meal with them and then offered to share his one double bed. The wife would sleep on the side nearest the stove, her husband would sleep in the middle and the bachelor would sleep on the far side. It seemed fair enough, but the wife had a hard time getting to sleep for fear she'd fall out of bed. She was awake when their host got up to shake down the stove and add more wood, the better to keep his guests warm. However, he'd forgotten to button the flap on his long underwear so there he was, his bare backside, inches from the nose of his female guest. The next day she told her husband about her nighttime vision and made him swear he'd never tell, but somehow the story got around.

One other thing to be noted about long underwear is that it never went away. When it had been patched beyond recognition, it was turned into underwear and blankets for babies, menstrual pads for women, and sometimes blankets for the whole family. Several mills in Canada would take scraps of woolen fabric and turn them into new blankets—rather ugly, gray, no-nonsense blankets—but they lasted forever and were cheap.

One day, a woman in the Nampa area of the Peace River country was washing all her woolen scraps and hanging them on the line, preparatory to sending them off to Winnipeg to be made into a blanket or two. Along came the bank manager who was there to check out the situation and see if they really needed the loan that they had applied for.

He took one look at the washing on the line, an assortment of rags and patches, went back to his office and approved the loan. From then on, the family joked that it was their clothes line of poverty that had ensured the farm's future.

A Lousy Life for Newcomers

In the days before pesticides and bathtubs and hot water that flowed out of taps, lice thrived among us. They were small gray-brownish parasites that liked nothing better than bare skin under long woolen underwear, there to live in peace and contentment as long as possible. If underwear wasn't handy, there were other spots they liked, children's hair being a favorite. Many a child of pioneers came home from school after a louse inspection by the teacher or community nurse with instructions to shampoo their hair with some awful concoction (kerosene and coal oil were favorites) and then comb it carefully to remove any remaining nits (lice eggs).

Estelle Barr remembered the process:

By the time supper was over, the snow (we had gathered it from outside) had melted and the delousing commenced. Mom placed the five of us in an assembly line and attacked us with the skill and vengeance of a professional executioner. One by one, she pushed each lousy head into a pan of coal oil and from there into a basin of warm soapy water, followed by several rinses, accompanying each application with such scratching and scrubbing we feared for our hides. Then she all but scalped us with a black tooth comb especially designed to extract any lice or nits which might have miraculously survived the stringent ordeal.

That was just the beginning of the process. The children then had to take off their underwear and squash any lice they found in them. This search-and-kill part of the process was fun for children but not so much fun for mom, who then had to boil the five suits of underwear, rinse them and somehow get them dry to wear next day.

Strenuous efforts were taken to keep the bugs at bay. Lice and log houses seemed to be made for each other. The many cracks in the logs, between the logs and between the wooden planks of the floor were perfect places for lice to lurk. Even if a woman managed to make her home louse free, their next visitor was liable to leave a new batch.

In *A Prairie Wife's Tale*, Shirley Keyes Thompson describes her battle of the bugs.

> We didn't realize at first the hopelessness of our task. Our arsenal included the use of every device known to the experts: fumigation, Black Flag (a bug killer), liquid poison for those bugs who drank, and powder for those who ate. We used everything but what we should have used, namely fire. Fire would have been used if we had had the money to rebuild.

James Minifie recalled that when he and his mother first saw their new house, they weren't entirely impressed. It was just a small unpainted brown shed on the edge of a Saskatchewan homestead, but James's father had built it entirely by hand and was very proud of it. So proud that when he discovered he was lousy after a trip to town the previous fall, he stripped down to the buff, threw his underwear over a fence post and jumped into a nearby slough to bathe before he entered his sweet home. It was fall and this naked romp must have been a cold shock to the system, but those were the measures people would take to avoid the pests. His underwear hung outside all winter, and by the time the family recovered the underwear the next spring, frost had taken care of any animal life.

Bedbugs were another challenge—the same problem and the same inadequate solutions. The Pyatt family, traveling by oxen and wagon in the Hardisty area of Alberta, stopped at a hotel en route to their homestead. As Estelle Barr describes it in "Louse Inspection," the wife saw bed bugs crawling on the bedroom wall so she "pinned them to the wall with my hat pins so the proprietor could see them." As if that weren't bad enough, she then spotted a grayback louse on her husband's shirt collar. She knew there'd be too many lice to pin down. When they got to their own place next morning, she put her husband's clothes into a tub of salt water to kill the lice. But even that ended badly. The cow got loose the next night and ate the underwear, lice and all.

One year, a farmer near Berwyn, Alberta, had a few extra dollars so he invested in a secondhand telephone. It was a big deal to have a phone in those days, but this one came with a bonus—bedbugs were alive and well within the phone itself and soon made themselves at home in their new dwelling. Edith Brong Frederickson tells the story in the local history *Brick's Hill, Berwyn and Beyond*:

Poor mother worked to exhaustion trying to get ahead of those pesky parasites but to little avail. No amount of spraying cracks and crevices with disinfectant, wall papering and calcimining could discourage the hateful things. If anything, mother's efforts just made them more virile.

Josephine Hitz of Dixonville, Alberta, bought a picture frame at an auction sale. She couldn't understand why she suddenly had an infestation of bed bugs in her house. They were in the picture frame.

Women were ashamed to be found with bugs of any sort in their lives, but men who worked outside weren't so particular. When Catherine Neil spent a summer in a sheep camp with her sheepherder husband, she was surprised to hear the men ask any visitors that came to the camp, "Are you lousy?" On one occasion, her brother-in-law told a pair of strangers, "You can't stop the night as my pals and I are lousy." The strangers replied, "Oh, don't trouble about that. My pal and I are the same."

One rather weak weapon in the battle against pests was the Saturday night bath. Bare skin was seldom let out of its wrappings in years past. The exception was the weekly bath, where every member of the family was expected to participate. Not that it could actually be called a bath. It was more like a brief encounter, a nodding acquaintance, with water. There was never much water, and what there was had to be shared with the whole family. Here's how R.F. Anderson of Bowden, Alberta, described his Saturday night bath:

Each family kitchen with its Congoleum-covered floor became the bath center for the household each Saturday night. The largest wash tub, usually a round galvanized one, was hauled in from the back porch or the woodshed, partly filled with soft rainwater when available and allowed to warm on top of the kitchen range. When it attained the right temperature, the tub was set in the middle of the kitchen floor and the bathing procedure commenced. It usually progressed from the youngest to the oldest of the children with Mother supervising the event, scrubbing backs or washing hair and seeing that there was no splashing. As each customer was completed, a few extra dippers of warm water from the reservoir at the back of the range were added to the tub so that when it was finally dad's turn to hop into the tub, there was a bit more water than when No. 1 child first fell afoul of the scrub brush.

Mother is not mentioned in the bath lineup. Logically she should have been second to last. But mother probably had herself a spit bath in the privacy of her bedroom. *Spit bath* was a euphemism for a quick wash with basin and face cloth.

Mike Kelly didn't worry about privacy—he was a trapper who lived alone in the mountains near Jasper, Alberta. In his diary on January 27, 1927, he wrote: "Had a wash day today. Washed everything but my face." Then he goes on to say, "Went up to marten tracks. No tracks. Am feeling pretty punk . . . am almost disgusted for sure. First time I ever felt lonesome in my life."

If he washed everything but his face, he might have washed his underwear. To do that, he would collect snow and melt

Why hasn't the bride stepped into this picture? Could this be an arranged marriage? Perhaps a mail-order bride got cold feet in this photo called "Prairie Wedding." There are no dates, no names with the picture. Staff at the Provincial Archives in Edmonton estimate it was taken about 1903.

But if you look carefully, there's more information. It certainly is a prairie wedding. Look at the horizon, look at the expanse of sky—two-thirds sky, one-third earth. Sometimes on the prairies there's nothing but sky, but this wedding day, there's just enough earth to stand on to be married. There are no buildings, no trees, no flowers—just earth and sky.

The priest is waiting beside an altar that looks like a few boxes covered with ecclesiastical cloths. He probably brings them with him as he travels the countryside, turning sod shacks, hillsides and prairies into places of worship. His Bible is ready.

So is the groom. There he stands, a sturdy man, dressed in his best suit—probably his only suit. On the ground beside him is his hat, his white forehead making plain that he seldom takes it off. It's the sign of farmers everywhere. It's cold. The women are wearing coats, shawls and kerchiefs, their babies wrapped up.

The men don't need as much on the outside because, inevitably, all of them, including the groom, are wearing their long johns.

Could the bride be considering whether or not to step into this picture? Has she got her binoculars out? Not likely. Women didn't have that kind of choice then. But the setting does look as if the arrangements were made quickly. No flowers, no pew bows. Just that forlorn chair standing out front, waiting for the bride to step into the frame, sit there and take her vows. Does she know about men? Does she know about long underwear that she'll have to sleep beside from now on, wash it until it falls apart, then make it into baby clothes? Does she know any of this? Or was it all done by mail? Perhaps she arrived on the train yesterday, and today there's a wedding. If that's the case, it's no wonder she hasn't stepped into the picture. It's all too fast, too cold and there's no music.

But there's no opting out now. The wedding awaits her. And in due time, she'll join the other women in the community in getting a church built for her children to be married in. There'll be houses to fill the huge silence in this bowl of sky and earth. And there might even be music. (COURTESY PROVINCIAL ARCHIVES OF ALBERTA)

And is this the bride awhile later? The same chair? The same flat earth all around? The same groom beside her, albeit a bit thinner? If it is, they've made a good start and the personal has become the practical. How to survive. (COURTESY GLENBOW ARCHIVES, NA-4340-1)

it on his stove before undressing and washing his underwear. Then he had to dry it on lines strung inside his lonely cabin. He couldn't hang it outside in January. No wonder he was feeling punk. He needed a wife.

Maybe he should have washed his face and sat down to write a letter.

Mail-Order Brides

The *Western Home Monthly* published out of Winnipeg had a popular feature called "Correspondence File." People could write in and ask for all sorts of things: recipes, farming information, a plow or even a wife, as the need arose. Sometimes there wasn't much difference between the plow and the wife. A letter in October 1906 outlined the writer's requirements for a wife:

Dear Editor . . . I am a prosperous young farmer with a half section of land fully equipped with horses and machinery and my ideas of a good wife run something as follows. She should be a good cook, willing to feed and look after the poultry, pigs, calves, milk about five cows, keep the house clean, do the washing, ironing, weed the garden and be prepared to get a lunch on the table for an occasional caller. Of course she could play the piano, go to town or mend the clothes in her spare time. Hoping you will be able to send me a photograph of a suitable young lady of dark complexion . . . A Home Lover.

Just when this hard-working woman was supposed to play the piano is not fully explained. Was the piano in the deal, or did she have to supply it herself? And what's in it for her? Home Lover doesn't mention that part of the deal, but it will likely involve babies and even more work. To be fair, she will get a home in the process, and that was enough for many women. Indeed, many of the men and women thus matched across the miles made good lives for themselves and their families. But it's interesting to note a letter to the "Correspondence File" in December 1905 from "A Young Widow" who presents another point of view.

I have read your correspondence column for the last few months with regard to the many favorable chances afforded women to secure husbands from among the farmers on the prairies. I have met some of these so-called farmers, many of whom live in huts and are hardly able to keep themselves, let alone keep a woman. They could keep her poor alright [sic]. Most of those chaps are seedy, chronic, poky, old swaybacks and about the only time they show a little life is when they get filled up with bad whiskey. Thanks. None of them gents for me.

Obviously, she's not convinced. But there were many men and women who did make wedding plans by long distance. So many young men had flocked to the prairies in search of land and opportunity in the late 1800s that there was an abundance of single men in the West and an overabundance of women in more settled areas. Something had to bring them together, and letters were better than nothing. That was not the case for the young woman who arrived by train in Fort Macleod in the early 1900s to meet the Mountie who had corresponded with her and eventually suggested marriage. She got off the train, but where was he? He who had pledged to "maintain the right" was on a nearby hillside checking her out with powerful binoculars. After several minutes of consideration, he decided she wouldn't do and sent his orderly with a note of regret and some money to get her back home again.

Eaton's Catalogue: For Necessities and for Dreams

Clifford Sifton, Minister of the Interior in the Laurier government of the late 1800s, invited the world to come to Canada and settle the West. He especially encouraged "stalwart peasants in sheepskin coats," because he wanted immigrants from Europe who could recognize good land when they saw it and plant crops and make communities. But those stalwart peasants had to have more than sheepskin coats to get the job done.

Mail-order catalogues were an absolute necessity, a cornerstone, in the development of the West. The homesteader out on a frozen plain could write up an order, walk through a blinding blizzard to the nearest post office, mail the order with a money order enclosed and wait for the goods to be sent a few weeks later. He'd then walk back, possibly through another blinding blizzard, to pick up his order. With any luck, he'd have ordered long underwear and could change into it right there and then in the post office before going back out again into the driving wind and snow.

Timothy Eaton established a general store in Toronto in 1869 and produced his first mail-order catalogue in 1884, a thirty-two-page booklet with straightforward descriptions and prices, no pictures. It was exactly what the thousands of small towns and rural communities of Canada needed. Men's underwear proved to be such a big seller that by 1889 the catalogue included an extensive list to choose from. There were still no pictures, just matter-of-fact descriptions of shirts and drawers that sold separately from fifty to sixty-nine cents each. A one-piece suit of underwear cost fifty to ninety cents, depending on whether you wanted wool or cotton. "Scotch Lambs Wool Non Shrinkable Shirts and Drawers, hand knitted and well finished" sold for between $2.50 and $4.75. This was probably too much money for the homesteader walking through the blizzard, but at least the choice was there.

By 1897 the catalogue was bigger and bolder, and included four line drawings of men in the underwear section looking somewhat asexual with no indication of male anatomy. Ten years later, all the underwear choices were illustrated with line drawings. Now you could tell whether your choice had shoulder seams and tight cuffs and other minor details, but you still couldn't see the back of the one-piece suits. There was no explanation about this part of the underwear other than the words, "open crotch." This signaled that the one-piece underwear had a flap in the back that must be folded and unfolded in the process of going to the bathroom. It wasn't until the catalogue moved into the 1920s that men were shown with a back as well as a front, by which time there was also mention of "closed crotch underwear."

Eaton's was first into the mail-order business in Canada. Judging by the number of times its mentioned in local history books, it was also first in the minds and hearts of Canadians. One west coast woman remembered her family referring to it as Timothy's Epistle to the British Columbians.

The catalogue was, in fact, something of a Bible, no offence intended. Women across the prairies looked to the catalogue as the last word in fashion. *So this is what they're wearing in the big cities this year.* Some sought health and happiness in the back pages among the medications and perfumes. *Maybe mother's health will improve with this tonic.* Men looked for motors, milking machines, pumps and machine parts. Even if they couldn't afford the parts, they got to see diagrams of the fixtures and sometimes figured out their own solutions. *Oh, that's how it's supposed to work.* Parents stocked up every spring and fall with new clothes for the kids, as many as they could afford at any rate. *Do I have to wear blue bloomers again this year? I hate them.* The catalogue even offered young people a bit of sex education in that they could look at bodies in underwear and try to figure out what went where. It was a book to dream on, to play the game of, *What would I have on this page, if I could have anything?*

The personal service that Eaton's offered was a great boon as well. Beth Creighton's father, a farmer far from town, didn't have a catalogue handy before his 1935 wedding, so he wrote to Eaton's personal shopper and asked for "one wedding ring, two pairs of underwear and a night shirt." And Eaton's came through, selecting the items and sending them COD.

The catalogue even made some dreams come true with its Christmas service: for a fee, the catalogue company sent gifts for children to be distributed at Sunday school or school concerts. Sometimes those gifts were the most exciting events in a child's life. At Christmastime too, girls who were lucky enough to have a new party dress each year usually got it from the catalogue. One year, Frances Ernst Walz was surprised to see four other girls in exactly the same dress as her new one at her Christmas concert. "This most beautiful dress happened to grace the front page of the special Christmas catalogue and it came in blue, red and green so there was a variation in colors, so we didn't mind at all," she wrote years later in *Sweaty Brows and Breaking Plows,* the Mayton-May City local history.

Even getting the parcels was exciting. Mable Mckenzie Dersch remembers:

> As soon as threshing was done every fall, a huge order was sent to the Timothy Eaton Company in Winnipeg for all the family clothing, all household linens, blankets, overshoes, shoes, etc. . . . It usually took two weeks for the Eaton order to come by freight and it came packed in huge wooden and cardboard boxes. What a gala time when it finally arrived. Nothing was opened until after the supper dishes were done and that was one night it didn't take long to get them done. Oh, the excitement of getting all our new things and waiting for each box to be opened to see what was in it.

A man in Fort Chipewyan, however, took the idea of catalogue ordering to the extreme. Eaton's catalogue came to that northern community in the early 1920s and it was a "big thing," according to Madeleine Bird in her memoir, *Living Kindness.* One man in particular was quite taken with the concept so he made out an order and sent it off. He checked the post office constantly, and when a box finally arrived, he said, "I didn't order a box. I ordered myself a woman, a wife and a pretty one. I didn't order this box." That was one customer for whom Eaton's could not guarantee satisfaction or money refunded.

Sometimes even the arrival of the new catalogue created problems. One mother in the Drumheller region had her children draw lots to see who would be first to look at it. And even when the catalogue ended up in the biffy a year later, there was still controversy. "I remember my mom giving me heck for taking too long out back, yet she used to take a lantern and an Eaton's catalogue and spend hours out there, it seemed to me," a pioneer from Rocky Mountain House remembered.

Eaton's also contributed to education. Grace Cunningham got her first teaching job in 1918 in Saskatchewan and found that only two of her students could speak English. So she borrowed some readers from another school and brought an Eaton's catalogue from home to help her students learn the language.

As times changed, so did the catalogue. There was heated criticism when the illustrations for women's underwear changed from drawings to photographs of actual women. One protest letter mentioned the "low necks and shoes with very little leather." Another pointed out that women were being fined in various parts of Canada for wearing shorts that didn't meet community standards, but Eaton's could go right ahead and advertise them for sale.

The men who ran Eaton's occasionally had a problem with the women who worked in the stores. Very early rules stated that women's skirts were never to rise so high that ankles were visible, and sleeves never to rise above elbow length. It was only after women began riding bikes to work in various locations and were ruining their long skirts on the bicycle chain that Eaton's relented and let them wear slightly shorter skirts. Blouses were not to be provocative—nothing that would cause men's eyes to drift. Colors were to be black, navy, or brown in winter, white in summer, but no patterned dresses. If a female clerk came dressed in anything that contravened the rules, she had to wear a black smock that day.

Eaton's got into hot water for what were called sweat-shop conditions and low pay for some of the manufacturing arms of the business, as well as for their bigoted hiring, anti-union policies and their stingy pay policies. But none of that affected their many loyal customers out on the prairies.

Between 1900 and 1910, close to one million immigrants sailed across the Atlantic to Canada—one million people in ten years, scattered across this huge country. Rev. J.S. Woodsworth said in 1909, "Within the past decade, a nation has been born . . . but how shall we weld this heterogeneous mass into one people? That is our problem."

Catalogues, not government programs or the church, were one small answer to the problem. They didn't discriminate, they didn't preach, they didn't cost anything. They treated everyone the same. In the pages of every eagerly awaited catalogue were the fulfillments of immigrants' dreams of a better life in a new world. Send your money, we'll send you the goods.

However, Eaton's can't take all the credit for uniting the country. There were other catalogue companies. Simpson's got into the mail-order business, head to head with Eaton's, in 1893. They were Eaton's biggest competitor, and even bigger after they merged with Sears of the United States in 1953. Though Sears eventually surpassed Eaton's in sales, they never quite got the respect and love that Eaton's garnered through the years. Two years after Eaton's gave up their catalogue business in 1976, Simpson's catalogue was taken over by Sears of Canada and still exists in various guises under that name. The Hudson's Bay Company also published a catalogue in 1896, about the same time as Eaton's and Simpson's, but only remained in the mail-order business until 1913. The Army and Navy catalogue also served customers from 1925 to 1986.

In British Columbia, Charles Woodward took up the idea of mail order. He opened a department store in Vancouver in 1892 and followed with a catalogue in 1897. Claiming to be "The Great Mail Order House of the West," the catalogue started off with the usual items—clothing, hardware and tools—but hit the jackpot when it began to offer food—groceries for people, hay and chicken feed for animals. That proved a great boon for settlers in remote areas of British Columbia and Alberta who couldn't always get to a store. Woodward's offer of pharmaceuticals by mail was also a hit with customers, but doctors and pharmacists fought that proposal tooth and nail. Woodward persevered, even to the extent of buying drugs from Eaton's and Simpson's to supply his customers. Woodward's published their main catalogue until 1953 and smaller catalogues into the 1970s.

Chapter 5
We Had Our Troubles

★　　★　　★　　★　　★

COME WITH ME TO THE COURTHOUSE IN RED DEER, Alberta, in March 1914. The proceedings over several days are only too typical of the troubles that women have experienced. First up before the judge on March 5 was Ross Piper, charged with seducing Miss May England. Piper admitted "wrongdoing" but claimed young May was fourteen at the time, which meant his wrongdoing wasn't a crime. By law, therefore, he wasn't guilty of seduction. No evidence was presented to show that the girl was not "of previous chaste character," but the jury still failed to agree upon a verdict. Case dismissed to a later date.

Next day Henry Norwest appeared in court charged with bigamy. Present were the two women who thought they were married to Henry, as well as the two men who had performed the services. Henry explained that he thought his first marriage was illegal having been performed without a license. "Some laughter was occasioned in court by the extreme naiveté of his replies to the cross-examination," the *Red Deer Advocate* reported. The newspaper account does not mention whether his wives were among those laughing. The jury took no time at all to find Henry guilty. The judge reserved sentence but told the court it would not be a heavy one, since he did not think there was "any great moral issue involved."

Then a Mr. Wagner appeared, charged with shooting a pig. Apparently the pig deserved what it got, having been a "great provocation." Mr. Wagner was fined five dollars and costs. A Mr. Fogelberg then pleaded guilty to forging a cheque. He was given a suspended sentence.

Then Mrs. Flynn was called to the courtroom. She was charged with the murder of her husband and child. Murray Anderson, a neighbor, began testimony about the accused, describing how he had gone to get his mail and met Mrs. Flynn. She had then told him, he said, that she had done it—killed her baby and her husband. During his testimony "the proceedings were dramatically interrupted by the prisoner fainting and on being somewhat revived, indulged in violent hysterics." What a terrible story must be behind that one. The murder charge was subsequently withdrawn, and Mrs. Flynn was committed to the Ponoka Mental Asylum.

Back to Ross Piper and the charge of seduction. The trial reconvened, and things looked bad for Mr. Piper when Dr. C.W. Sanders testified that Miss England was pregnant and that the timing was about right. But Mrs. Piper testified that it wasn't her husband but another man who had got May into trouble that night in the bushes. Mrs. Piper testified at length about one Harry Allen who, she said, met May in his room at the Great West Hotel. Harry Allen,

however took the stand to, emphatically deny having any "improper relations."

Red Deer folk must have had a lot to talk about for a few days. May England knew exactly what night the improper relations took place because Mrs. Piper had had a baby a few days after May's encounter in the bush and May had made note of the date. But Mr. Piper trumped her allegation with testimony from a member of the Orange Lodge who testified that Piper had been at Lodge that night. His name was on the attendance roster. How could he have been in the bushes with May? How indeed, but that unexpected piece of evidence didn't impress the jurors who brought in a verdict of guilty. Piper was sentenced to fifteen months with hard labor in the Lethbridge jail. "The judge remarked his satisfaction with the verdict of the jury," according to the *Advocate.*

The judge may have been satisfied, but what happened to the two women in this case—the real victims? Mrs. Piper was on her own looking after a new baby. Fourteen-year-old May England was expecting one. How did they manage? Was May shunned by her family and by other more respectable women? Did she go to the Beulah Home in Edmonton to deliver the baby and give it up for adoption, never to know the child's whereabouts? For her part, was Mrs. Piper invited to the next Ladies Aid tea? Could she hold up her head in the community? Not likely, not for a while. In fact, the lives of both women would have been affected for a very long time, all because they were female and had the body parts that result in the continuation of the race. Having a female body at times seemed like one trouble after another.

Speaking of trouble, the word *trouble* was one of the most frightening a woman could hear in years gone by. If she was *in trouble*, it meant she was pregnant outside marriage. A big sin and big trouble. God and society allowed sexual relations between married folk, that's all. Anything else was forbidden. In fact, there were so many warnings about sex before marriage that one has to wonder if young newly married couples enjoyed the sexual act all.

Options for the women who got into trouble and wouldn't or couldn't marry the man were limited. Seek an abortion? More or less impossible in earlier times. Go to visit an aunt and come back slimmer four months later? That happened a fair amount, and the children left behind in the orphanages had to make their own way through society's expec-

tations, sometimes an unmentionable journey. Stay within the community and face up to the music? That choice was a hard one. Have the baby in some faraway place and turn to prostitution? After all, sex got you into this mess. Let sex get you out? Yes, sometimes that was the choice.

The Slur of Illegitimacy

Kate Simpson Hayes belonged in the twentieth century, maybe even the twenty-first, instead of the nineteenth. She married Charles Simpson in 1882, bore him two children and left him when it turned out he wasn't much good. Leaving your husband was taboo. As was divorce. She decided to skip divorce anyway. It was expensive (at least $1,000, a huge amount in the late 1800s), and to obtain one required an act of Parliament. Furthermore, there was such social stigma about divorce that most people just moved out and got on with their lives as Simpson Hayes did. She did change the order of her name, re-adopting her maiden name as her last name, keeping Simpson as the middle one.

She relocated to Regina and became an active participant in the cultural activities of the city. There she met Nicholas Flood Davin, a lawyer and publisher of the *Regina Leader*. Davin was a dashing newspaperman who could charm the birds out of the trees. He scored the coup of the century when he talked himself into Louis Riel's jail cell on the eve of his hanging and got an exclusive interview. Simpson Hayes was bright, independent, forthright. They fell for eachother.

Considering the state of birth control in the late 1800s, it was inevitable that Kate twice became pregnant and twice managed to be out of town during the final months of pregnancy. The son was taken into private care. Not a word got out about the birth. When the daughter was born two years later, she was put in a Roman Catholic orphanage. Again, not a word. It wasn't until the daughter, Agnes, became an adult and started to ask questions that the unhappy tale almost came out. Davin had eventually married—but not to Kate—and his new wife agreed to take both the children. The son was found and claimed as a "nephew," but the daughter was lost in a maze of conflicting records and stories.

By then Kate was living in Winnipeg and writing an advice column for the local paper, a sort of Ann Landers of her day. One day a woman wrote asking for advice about the shame of a pregnancy outside marriage. Kate Hayes responded:

Well, my girl, you are face to face with a problem which began in the Garden of Eden . . . and has been going on . . . being enacted over and over again. Well, you must struggle back to the old road, the road of Right doing, Right thinking, Right acting . . . and whatever you do, do your duty to your child.

How galling that must have been for her own illegitimate children, especially for Agnes, who by now had discovered the identity of her mother. But not once did Kate admit to it. She hinted at it, occasionally supported Agnes financially, signed some of her letters "M," but she actually never said the words, "You are my daughter." In fact, in her last letter to Agnes, her daughter who so desperately wanted to be recognized, she said, "I will not be written to in any such tone by anybody much less by you for whom I have done all that was possible, under the circumstances."

Constance Maguire has described pregnancy outside of marriage as the "slur of illegitimacy." Kate Simpson Hayes may have been able to change her name, but she couldn't change her attitude or society's. She was a product of her time when illegitimacy—now known as single motherhood—was just not acceptable. It wasn't proper, and if it occurred, it should stay secret.

You're in Trouble? Too Bad!

"I'm in trouble," were the most frightening words possible for a girl to say years ago. They meant that you were pregnant, and the man who had promised to marry you "if anything happened" wouldn't honor his word. You were going to be disgraced, thrown out of your home perhaps, laughed at, sent to visit an aunt, scarred for life. Your mother cried, your father wouldn't look at you, the church turned its back, the teachers looked away. All because some man sweet-talked you into intercourse, which, because it was illicit and hurried and perhaps the first experience for both of you, was not worth a lifetime of regret.

This shunning and disgrace of girls who became pregnant outside of marriage was patently unfair. The experience was so deep, so disgraceful, that some girls commited suicide rather than own up to their "trouble." Or they ran away from home and lived awful lives because they had made one mistake. In the meantime, the man was fine. His buddies gave him knowing looks, his life proceeded as planned—unless the girl's father forced a shotgun wedding, telling the guilty man he must marry or else. In most cases the shotgun wasn't actually necessary. But marriage was if reputations were to be salvaged. A quick wedding would take place, the old ladies in the neighborhood would mark the wedding date on their calendars and the countdown would begin.

When the baby came too soon after the wedding, it was explained as a premature birth, but everyone knew. "Look at him, he's a good eight pounds if an ounce. That's not premature," people would whisper. So the secret always got out. But at least the child didn't have to live with the label "bastard"—the label for a mother's unmentionable behavior.

Sometimes the pregnant girl managed to hide her condition for many months thanks to gathered skirts and aprons. There's one amazing story from northern Alberta about a church camping weekend with boys, girls, chaperones and preachers along. Boys were in tents on one side of the camp, girls on the other. Suddenly, in the middle of the night, there was a commotion in one of the girls' tents. When the chaperones investigated, they discovered a girl having a baby. No one even knew she was pregnant. She had hidden her secret all those months. Perhaps she thought the whole thing would go away like a bad dream if she just denied what was happening. What else could she do? There were so few options besides disgrace and shame.

This story, however, may have had a happy ending. When the preacher found out about the baby, he decided he'd get a father for the new mother right then, that night. He went from tent to tent in the boys camp. "Will you marry so-and-so?" he asked each of the boys, and finally one agreed. The horses were hitched, the preacher and new family drove to the nearest town the next day and the marriage took place. It must have been a huge surprise for the families of both bride and groom, but at least there was a marriage certificate. That made the situation all right—sort of.

Even a marriage certificate couldn't guarantee respectability. A man and a woman in Edmonton discovered the woman was about four months pregnant. They got married secretly and then made up some excuse to go to the United States for a while. There the baby was delivered and given up for adoption. Even though they were married, they could not bring home the child of their love before marriage without disapproval. No one knew

about the whole episode until many years later when the couple had both died. That's when one of the surviving legitimate sons (there had been three more children) received a phone call one day from a man in the United States who said, "I think I am your brother." And sure enough, he was. A full brother. They have since connected, and everything's fine. But one can't help thinking of the despair that must have lay behind the decision to leave the child behind because of the shame and shunning that awaited young people who "sinned."

In another town, a mother and teenage daughter suddenly left town to visit relatives. When they came back five or six months later, mother had a new baby and teenage daughter went back to school. There was lots of talk and knowing looks, but the family stuck to their story and raised two daughters instead of one.

Most major cities had a "Beulah" or "rescue" home of some sort, where pregnant single women could live (and work) for a few months until their babies were born. Most women would sign their babies over to the government, hope they'd be adopted by a good family and head back to their hometowns or back to their jobs or back to whatever awaited them. That would be the last they saw or knew of their child unless years later there was a phone call that began something like this: "Hello, this is Parent Find calling. We think we have found your child, and we wonder if you wish to be identified."

Oh, Give Me a Home . . .

Many social problems in the first half of the twentieth century were solved—or at least tackled—by the provision of "homes." There were homes for orphans and abandoned children, homes for bad girls, homes for bad boys, homes for the insane, homes for the indigent. The only category that seems to be missing is homes for the elderly, which is easily explained by the fact that in those days the elderly stayed at home.

Most of the homes of an earlier era were established by church or charitable organizations that set their own rules about who was good and who was bad and what should be done about them. Sometimes the rules were draconian with a good deal of righteous judgment thrown in for good measure. The Mountview Residential Girls Home in Calgary made their charges wear bloomer suits, a combination of a middy top with big, floppy bloomers. Whenever the girls left the home, everyone could identify them as "bad girls from that home" because of their distinctive outfits.

What had these girls done? By modern standards, not much. They had run away from home, stolen, skipped school, hung around with unsavory characters or sassed their elders. Sometimes a particularly hard case had done all of the above. She'd be a candidate for the home for a period of time, where school attendance would be supervised and curfews imposed, where she would have to help with household chores and attend Sunday school classes.

If the girl in question had merely run away and skipped school for a few days, she'd be lectured sternly by the female child worker and told to go home and behave. Lecturing seemed to work rather well. Sometimes wayward girls were placed with foster families whose morals and example the social workers had approved. Decisions about who should be in foster care depended on the judgment of the child worker.

If all else failed, police were brought in to pick up a wayward girl under an official charge of vagrancy. The vagrancy law, vague enough to cover most problems, stated that any boy or girl who contravened a municipal, provincial or federal law, or was guilty of sexual immorality or a similar form of vice, was

The All People's Mission in Winnipeg was established by the Methodist Church to serve needy children and adults under the banner of "Social Gospel." Theirs was the first orphanage in the West. (COURTESY UNITED CHURCH OF CANADA ARCHIVES, CONFERENCE OF MANITOBA & NORTHWESTERN ONTARIO)

a vagrant and therefore could be charged or picked up and placed somewhere. In Calgary a female might end up in the Home for Fallen Women. Those words actually graced the sign of a Calgary building in the 1930s. One of the first things Herb Allard did when he joined that city's social welfare department was insist that the sign come down. Some years later, when Allard became Chief Justice of the Family Court in Calgary, he could have ordered the sign taken down, but in the early days he had to talk long and hard to get it removed. There were fallen women and there were upright women, and the sign told it like it was.

Children who ended up at the All People's Mission in Winnipeg were not there because of anything they did. It was their folks who had problems, so the youngsters were brought to the Mission and cared for, thanks to the Methodist Church's emphasis on "social gospel" that began in the late 1800s. Believing it was as important to do good works as to talk about them, Methodists established homes wherever they were needed and whenever they had the money. Eventually, municipal and provincial agencies assumed responsibility for most of these homes, but for a while in western Canada, they were the sole resource for orphans or abandoned children, who

were lucky indeed if they ended up in a charity-affiliated home.

And who can criticize that? Somebody had to help the unfortunate in the days before governmental safety nets were established. At least the children in the homes were warm and clothed and fed. Their mothers or fathers were dead, or looking for work in another part of Canada, or were poor and sick. Often they were recent immigrants, many of whom didn't have jobs or money or winter clothes. Maybe they had just given up. In the story of immigration, the first generation didn't always make it, but they left behind children who did. Or did they? For example, it would be interesting to find out who the children in the picture are and what became of them. How many managed to get on? How many had to wait for the next generation to see improvement? An orphan explained his situation thus: "What happened to my father? I really don't know. He went to work in the mines in Ontario and we lost him."

The All People's Mission was one of the first and most famous of all the western Canadian homes. Established in the 1890s in the poorest neighborhood of Winnipeg, it was proof that the church cared about the people in its midst. It would help those who needed it most—in this case, the children. The superintendent for many years was J.S. Woodsworth, who went on to establish the Cooperative Commonwealth Federation (CCF), now morphed into the New Democratic Party of Canada.

The most unmentionable places were the homes or asylums for those with mental and physical disabilities. The silence was especially deep about people labeled as suffering from mental disabilities. They were viewed as a disgrace to the family, a stain that could not be talked about. A doctor and his wife in a small Alberta town had a child who was injured during birth. The family kept him in an upstairs room, and Lottie, the hired girl, used the back stairs to go up and down to care for him. He was a beautiful child according to the very few relatives who saw him, but he had to be kept out of sight. He was unmentionable. Why? Because he had brain damage and would never develop normally. After Lottie died, he ended up in the asylum in Ponoka, Alberta, an institution that opened in 1911 as the Hospital for the Insane but was renamed in 1924 as the Provincial Mental Hospital.

Medical care didn't exist for those who couldn't pay for it. So when Thelma, child of a poor family from the southern United States, fell from her high chair and lost her hearing, nothing could be done. She was deaf from then on. At age nineteen, she married a much older man, and in 1908 they moved to western Canada to take up a homestead in the Vermilion area. After the birth of her sixth child, Thelma had a breakdown. Now it would be called post-partum depression, but then it was simply called crazy. She was admitted to Ponoka for treatment, which must have helped, because she came home for a few years and had one more child.

Suffering from depression once more, she was readmitted to Ponoka. She never saw her family again. Considered a quiet, well-behaved patient who required little or no treatment, she was eventually moved from Ponoka to an auxiliary hospital in Claresholm. There she spent her last days, working in the kitchen and the garden. Other women at the same facility worked in the sewing room and made all the clothing for the inmates except shoes, stockings and brassieres.

Neither institution has any records documenting Thelma's condition or treatment. She couldn't hear, she didn't have sign language, she couldn't read or write. It's fortunate that there was a place where she could be cared for, but it was custodial care only. There were no programs to enrich her life. The cruelest thing of all must have been the loss of her family. Mental illness was so shrouded in shame that her family didn't even speak of her, let alone see her. It was as if she had never existed.

It took a third generation to seek out her story and find her grave in Claresholm. The marker is a standard concrete and tin plaque supplied by the government. Her family hadn't even known she'd been moved from Ponoka.

Babies for Export

"Babies for Export" was a phrase heard a lot in Alberta in the late 1940s when something of a social conscience was aroused about orphans or wards of the government and their adoption. The entire process was dealt with by the Child Welfare Branch of the Department of Public Welfare, which meant that everything was handled more or less by one government department and one man, C.B. Hill. He had the power to decide that one baby would go to a family in the United States, while another would go to the small town of Peoria in the Peace River country and so on. There's no question that he did a pretty good job of picking and choosing, but the system was very casual.

Prospective parents had only to fill in a form and declare that they were good people for a child to arrive shortly thereafter. If the adoption was an Alberta one, local authorities might verify the economic situation of the prospective parents, but in rural areas, the checks were not always done. If the child was going out of Canada to the United States, Guatemala, San Salvador or Costa Rica (Alberta children went to all those countries) no formal follow-up occurred. The Alberta authorities depended on the references supplied in the applications. By 1947 some 243 babies had traveled south into the unknown. The department reported that letters did come from some of the families—and eventually from some of the adopted children—with glowing reports. Nonetheless, it was a risky way of managing the process.

The Alberta chapter of the women's service club known as the Imperial Order Daughters of the Empire (IODE) hired Charlotte Whitton to come to Alberta to determine what was happening to our babies. Whitton, then an Ottawa social worker and later mayor of Ottawa, criticized the government for some of its systems or lack of systems. She reported that the superintendent was far too powerful, that local jurisdictions didn't work with provincial ones, that women were more or less forced to

All the children in this picture from the Beulah Home in Edmonton were adopted by families in the Peoria district of northern Alberta. The adoptive mothers with their children are, left to right, Viola Yanke holding Betty; Lil Berg holding Bernadine with Delvin and Kelly standing in front; Goldie Comm holding Connie; Alfreda Seibel with Bonnie Rae in front and Ralph beside her; Mrs. Bennett with Alice standing in front of Ralph Seibel; Florence Taylor standing in front of Mrs. Bennett, (Mrs. Taylor could not be there for the picture); Mrs. Davis holding Winn with Virginia in front of her; Nina Rude with Rodney. (COURTESY ALICE FORTIER, GRANDE PRAIRIE)

give their babies up for adoption, that workers should be trained in child psychology and should be better paid, that it would be better to support poor families instead taking their children away, and more. She didn't mince words and created quite a stir. Alberta fought back against Whitton's findings with its own commission. Once the dust had settled, social work systems were overhauled. Babies no longer were sent out of the country, and supervision and the adoption process improved.

Families from Peoria in northern Alberta adopted fifteen babies. The first two went to women who visited the orphanage connected to the Beulah Home in Edmonton. One woman chose a two-and-a-half-year-old boy for herself and a one-and-a-half-year-old boy for her sister, Lill, back in Peoria. A few days later, the women remembered that Lill had asked for a baby. So back they went back to the orphanage to exchange the one-and-a-half-year-old for a baby. As they were walking away with the baby, leaving the one-and-a-half-year old behind, he cried out to them, "Take me, mommy, take me."

Heartbreaking as that story is, it was the beginning of an amazing adoption story. Two years later, Lill decided she'd like another child. This time she wrote to the Beulah Home and a nurse brought the baby by train, handed her over and got back on the train. Another family sent for two girls. This time the nurse got off the train with two babies in her arms, a nametag pinned to each.

Years later, the adoptees in Peoria wrote their memoirs in a book, *Adoptees are Angels.* They all spoke warmly about their folks, that is, the people who adopted them and brought them up, but most sought out their birth parents in later years. There they found stories of mothers who weren't married, had no money and couldn't keep them due to the moral climate of the day. The grown children weren't so much interested in the reasons for their adoption as they were alternately thrilled and scared, excited and anxious to meet their birth relatives, especially their birth mothers. And they said again and again that meeting their birth relatives did not take away one bit from the love and gratitude they had for their adoptive families.

The Battle from Rubber Boots to Condoms

"If you could only tell me how to prevent conception, you would make me the happiest woman in Canada," wrote a nineteen-year-old Saskatchewan woman who was married with one baby and another on the way. She was writing to Margaret Sanger of New York, a woman who fought long and hard to make birth control available to women. For her trouble, she was spat upon in the streets and denounced from pulpits. It was a mean one-sided fight, this fight for the knowledge of contraception.

Perhaps the young woman quoted above is not the best example of someone desperately needing contraceptive information. She was expecting only her second child. Jean Browne, Saskatchewan's first public health nurse, knew more poignant tales. She once visited the home of a new Canadian family, poor as church mice, eight children, the husband in steady work but with very low pay:

When the little mother opened the door and saw me, she put her head on my shoulder and began to sob. She was pregnant again and, between sobs, she told me in her imperfect English that it was almost more than she could do to look after her eight children and she didn't know how she could manage another.

Meanwhile, legislators and decision-makers prattled on about the sanctity of the home, the holy state of matrimony and women's higher calling as mothers. "The hand that rocks the cradle rules the world" was a favorite old saw, but it wasn't true. Too many women didn't have time to rock the cradle let alone rule the world.

Until the 1950s in western Canada, the battle to disseminate contraceptive information was quiet, but it was fought astutely. The Good Cheer Club of Calgary made baby clothes for women who didn't have any, and while they visited with their gifts, they had a word or two about "other things." One annual report stated that a couple who had had four children, one after the other, was visited by a Good Cheer member and a representative of the Birth Control Society. Several years later, the annual report mentioned that the same family was in "no further need of layette assistance."

If contraceptive advice was given, the Good Cheer Club wasn't telling. Birth control devices were illegal, and so was the distribution of birth control information. Women tried, goodness knows. In 1929, the Saskatchewan women's branch of the United Farmers of Canada passed a resolution asking the national government to rescind the ban on dis-tributing birth control information. They were unsuccessful. Nevertheless, birth control clinics were organized in Ontario, Manitoba and British Columbia. Though there were murmurs from the churches and the chattering classes, the clinics managed to give advice and devices to some women. In Winnipeg, Mary Speechley organized her city's first Birth Control Society in 1934 and started out with a bang by getting permission to have the inaugural meeting in the Manitoba Legislative Building. Letters to the editor and protests to politicians forced Speechley and her group to retreat and hold meetings surreptitiously in their homes.

But Speechley didn't give up. She connected with A.R. Kaufman of Kitchener, Ontario. Kaufman was a most unlikely ally in the birth control battles. He was a wealthy manufacturer of rubber products including rubber boots and condoms. He was also a pragmatist. He could see that women were having more babies than they and government services could afford or manage. By the time he took an interest in the cause, there were several birth control clinics in major eastern cities (the first one was in Hamilton) and he helped them with money and supplies. But he could see they were attracting

THE ALBERTAN, Wednesday, December 6, 1978

She's ending 40 years of silence and fear

TORONTO (CP) — When 28-year-old Dorothea Palmer Ferguson was on trial in 1937 for dispensing birth control information and devices to women in a small village outside Ottawa, she told her lawyer she was ready to go to jail if her work was not considered philanthropic.

Mrs. Ferguson, 70, said Wednesday that after 40 years of silence since her acquittal of the charges on March 17, 1937, she wanted "to tell a few things that didn't get into the newspapers at the time."

Mrs. Ferguson of Ottawa said her case probably was the first in Canada to raise the defence of the public good as an answer to a charge of disseminating information on birth control.

Mrs. Ferguson was charged under Section 207 of the Criminal Code. The section was removed by an act of Parliament in 1968.

In the 1930s and up until the change in the Code, anyone disseeminating birth control information or articles to prevent conception was liable to two years' imprisonment.

Mrs. Ferguson, who used her maiden name Dorothea Palmer in her work to protect her husband's family, was hired as a nurse-social worker for the Parents' Information Bureau, based in Kitchener, Ont., to visit known low-income homes.

She received information on her prospective clients from doctors, social agencies, relief officers and clergymen.

She would visit these people, give them a certain amount of elementary information where necessary and, when asked, take an application for contraceptives.

But her work soon was discovered by certain groups, including the Roman Catholic church, which disagreed with birth control under any circumstances.

Mrs. Ferguson was arrested on Sept. 14, 1936, as she was leaving the home of a French Roman Catholic family. The family was on relief and there were 10 children.

The Crown called 21 women as witnesses, Mrs. Ferguson recalls. All of them were Catholics, all but one were FrenchCanadian.

In a record of the trial, the Crown attorney argued that it was not in the public good for a social worker to place Catholic women in a position to exercise birth control without warning them that it might be contrary to the teachings of their church. Mrs. Ferguson said one woman who asked her to visit had 22 children and was desperate.

"Her last two had been born blind. In that case, the husband was in a home for the insane because he had syphilis. But each time he was released he would impregnate his wife."

Mrs. Ferguson said that during the trial, she was taunted and verbally abused by men and women.

"After the trial was over, and I was acquitted, I was beaten up by a husband of one of the women who said he wanted to rape me," she said. "But he got my knee and a punch from my fist instead."

The Crown appealed the acquittal, but on June 2, 1937, the appeal was dismissed. So why did she go into virtual hiding for 40 years?

"My husband was ve[ry] much against me continu[ing] the work and we had quit[e a] few battles about it," M[rs.] Ferguson said. "I was still [in] fear for myself after [the] many threats and the [at]tempted rape."

"We had to sell our libra[ry] business and moved aw[ay] from Ottawa for a few yea[rs.] Luckily no one knew [my] married name as I h[ad] worked as a social work[er] and was charged under [my] maiden name."

Mrs. Ferguson said wit[h a] laugh that by coming ou[t of] hiding, "I am showing tha[t I] am finally of the age of d[is]cretion. Or maybe it's [my] Welsh pigheadedness."

DOROTHEA PALMER FERGUSON AT 70

Dorothea Palmer was so traumatized by her birth control trial in 1937 that she didn't speak publicly about it for forty years. (Calgary Albertan, December 6, 1978)

middle-class women, not the women who needed birth control the most. So he hired nurses to approach women in their homes. In the home, with permission, the nurses would discuss birth control strategies and leave a kit of J, N and C supplies—*J* for jelly, *N* for nozzle, and *C* for condom. This method wasn't as reliable as the diaphragm or pessary, but it was better than nothing. Kaufman's nurses often succeeded where birth control clinics failed because supplies of J, N and C were delivered to the door. Diaphragms had to be fitted by a doctor, a visit to the doctor cost money, and diaphragms were also a bother to use. Under businessman Kaufman's effective plan, the nurses were paid a commission. They were the Avon ladies of birth control, and they did good work.

Eventually, authorities charged one of Kaufman's nurses with dispensing birth control information in contravention of the Criminal Code. Dorothea Palmer, then of Eastview, Ontario, was arrested in September 1936 as she left the home of a large Roman Catholic family. She testified later at the trial that the woman in question, a mother of ten children, had telephoned and asked her to visit. But that didn't matter. Talk of birth control was not allowed.

During Palmer's trial, she told the court of another woman with twenty-two children who was desperate for help. "Her last two had been born blind. In that case, the husband was in a home for the insane because he had syphilis. But each time he was released, he would impregnate his wife," she testified. The jury acquitted Palmer of all charges. A legal loophole determined her actions to have been in the "public good and without excess."

The *Calgary Herald* did not carry a word about this important trial. Through October 1936 to February 1937 there wasn't a single editorial or other mention of the proceedings in Eastview. On February 13, 1937, the *Herald* did run several stories about rumors that the Dionne quintuplets were kidnap targets. The quintuplets were often featured in articles and advertisements, and they were certainly bigger news than birth control. Only on March 18, when Palmer was acquitted of all charges, did the *Herald* publish a small picture and story.

After the trial, Palmer disappeared from public view. She "had had enough," she said, after being subjected to insults and threatened with rape and abuse by both men and women in the community. She and her husband sold their business and moved away, but for the women who supported her at the time the verdict "was like winning the Grey Cup," she said. She didn't tell her full story until forty years later.

The Palmer trial was very important in the history of birth control in Canada. Suddenly, contraception wasn't unmentionable. In 1936, the United Church General Council approved the principle of voluntary parenthood, a phrase that sounded better than birth control. They even agreed to the establishment of voluntary parenthood clinics under public control and supervised by provincial health officers.

Kaufman became the father of birth control as it were, and was asked to establish his visiting nurse system in other Canadian cities. In the late 1930s, some fifty to seventy-five of his nurses were spreading the word. Slowly, more local birth control centers were set up—with advice and assistance from Kaufman if needed. So, if you were brave, of the right religion, lived in a city that had a clinic, had enough money to get a street car ticket downtown, were not embarrassed and not worried about having an internal exam, you could get sound birth control information and a referral to a doctor for the fitting of a diaphragm.

To avoid prosecution, doctors could describe the diaphragm as necessary for "gynecological support" or something similar. Available information was disseminated through the mail in plain brown envelopes. Still, many women did not or could not avail themselves of the services. "We took what we got because we couldn't do anything about it," is how Ella Shannon of Red Deer put it. Catholic women certainly couldn't do anything about it. They were told to obey their husbands and that childbirth was a cross they had to carry, just as Jesus had to carry his. But Madeleine Bird (a good Catholic who attended a Catholic residential school) did murmur a small protest: "Jesus didn't carry a cross all his life, pregnant," she said.

Where Are My Children?

By 1918 all the western provinces had film censor boards whose members watched every movie scheduled for public viewing. They had complete control and could cut any of the following: scenes portraying white slavery (unless a moral lesson was somehow conveyed); scenes involving gruesome bloodshed or corpses; drunkenness; notorious characters; drug addiction; poisoning; robbery; pick pocketing; the use of ether or chloroform; counterfeiting;

When this movie came to a Calgary theater in June 1918, it was advertised as "a strong warning to unwary young girls against the 'suasive lures of a class of young men." Men and women could not attend the movie together so there were separate showings.

(Courtesy Calgary Herald)

brutal treatment of children or animals; the ridicule of races, classes or religions; immodest dancing; needless exhibition of women in lingerie; husbands and wives in the same bed; sensual kissing and lovemaking; profanity; and vampires. In other words, all the elements of movies today.

At first their job was easy—cut a word here, remove the glimpse of a woman's leg there, ban the entire movie if necessary. But then filmmakers began packaging their products as "educational" and "important moral lessons," and the censors had a tougher time. A movie called *Where Are My Children?* came to the Liberty Theatre in Calgary in 1918. The half-page advertisement in the *Calgary Herald* described it as "the most amazing, most impressive, most dignified, yet most sensational production of its character in the history of Moving Pictures."

What was this amazing moving picture about? Well, sex—sort of. It tells the story of an innocent girl led into the sin of fornication by a cad who professes to love her. She becomes pregnant, suffers every kind of shame and anguish, and decides to obtain an abortion. Her death ensues—as do the hankies throughout the theater.

Why did the censors worry? The

story reinforces all the necessary messages of those times: see what results from playing around, see the shame it brings, see the awful fate it leads to. But sex lay under the story. The mere mention of sex might corrupt men and women, sending them out into the street eager to have sex themselves.

In order to prevent the banning of the film, the moviemakers cleverly turned it into a medical lecture. Advertisements proclaimed it as such strong stuff that men and women had to see it separately. In addition, nurses were on hand during the showings for both men and women to answer questions and provide pamphlets (for a charge) with further information. It was masterful marketing. The result was sold-out houses.

The film reviewer for the Calgary paper opined:

> It is one film which every woman and girl should see. Alberta is the first province in Canada to permit of it being shown and the picture justifies the action of the censor. The most fastidious on the questions of life can find no fault and the law provides that it must be shown only to segregated audiences, while boys and girls of ten-

der age must be accompanied by parents or guardians.

Not everyone agreed. When *Her Unborn Child,* another thinly disguised sex-with-a-message movie, came to Calgary, one of the local ministers weighed in to protest the handbills that had been distributed throughout the city. The advertisement stated that the movie revealed "the truth about birth control" and that's what got the minister upset. He wrote:

> I beg to enclose a copy of advertisement delivered openly at my door today which my wife brought to me with indignation . . . I denounce the circulation of an advertisement of this kind broadcast as an offence against decency and a breach of public morals.

Yet the movie delivered the sort of message that most ministers would approve of—that unnatural birth control led to childlessness, which led to an unhappy old age, misery, poverty and abandonment.

Eugenics: The Science that Wasn't

In most western towns, men in the know could go into the drugstore, wink at the druggist (a man of course), and the druggist would slip a package of condoms over the counter. No words needed. And women? They didn't discuss such matters. Anything to do with sex was unmentionable, which makes it even more surprising that the so-called science of eugenics got many people in western Canada talking about sex.

Not that sex was ever mentioned. Eugenics came in a package labeled "science" and was discussed as if men and women weren't really involved. It was all about the "fit" and the "unfit," who should be allowed to reproduce and who shouldn't. As animal husbandry, it made sense. Farmers knew how to produce a healthy herd by culling the less fit cows and keeping the best ones for breeding. But people aren't cows, and many of the people called unfit suffered from environmental influences such as poverty and disease. However, because newcomers without money, language or skills were crowding into western Canada in the early 1900s, words like the following found support:

> Positive eugenics demand that, in every way possible by education, agitation and legislation, we promote and encourage the marriage

of normal young people and the increase in the size of the family on the part of the more desirable elements of society. . . .Negative eugenics occupies itself with such education and legislation as would tend to decrease the marriage of degenerates and still further toward those measures that look toward a decrease in the size of the family in those questionable and defective human beings who are already married and still further to bring about either the segregation or sterilization of all members of society who are definitely, unmistakably and eugenically unsound, defective and tainted.

Mary Ries Melendy, MD, PhD, wrote these words in her 1904 book *The Science of Eugenics*. The popular book went through many updated editions. Notice her credentials. Sir Francis Galton, the originator of this dubious science, also had a great many credentials. He was a cousin of Charles Darwin, which gave him immediate credibility. Everyone recognized and respected Darwin's name, and if Darwin's cousin said that there were good and bad stock in the human herd and that some of them should not reproduce, it must be science. What was underneath all the big words, however, was sterilization of less-than-perfect men and women so that they could not reproduce and pass on their alleged feeblemindedness or criminal tendencies.

The whole appalling concept did manage to put the idea of "birth control" into circulation. But in the case of the eugenic theory, it was birth control intended for the "unsound, defective and tainted," not for women who wanted some control over their reproductive lives. Today, we understand eugenics to be wholly judgmental and unscientific, but at the time, it appealed to some as reasonable, new and scientific. Some of our national leaders bought into it, at least for a while. In Manitoba, CCF founder J.S. Woodsworth suggested Canada was indeed getting too many immigrants of "inferior stock" and recommended a more restrictive immigration policy based on eugenic principles. In Alberta, Emily Murphy saw too many women in her courtroom made miserable by too many children, poverty and ignorance. She spoke out vehemently on behalf of the idea of improving the genetic stock of the population to cut down on some of the misery. Finally, the United Farmers of

Alberta, the province's governing party, incorporated eugenics principles into law in 1928, making legal the sterilization of those judged to have mental disabilities. British Columbia passed similar legislation in 1933. A total of thirty-three states in the United States had already enacted similar legislation.

Alberta did not repeal this law until 1972. By then, 2,822 Albertans had been sterilized for reasons varying from possessing a low IQ to apparent promiscuity.

Another Awful War

Although the world had already fought a war that was supposed to end all wars, Canadian men and women went to war again from 1939 to 1945. Some 43,000 women left hearth and home to serve overseas as auxiliaries to the army, air force and navy. They didn't serve in combat roles, but served behind the lines as stenographers, drivers, mechanics, pilots and cipher clerks. Most of their training occurred on the job once they were posted, but before they left they had to attend birth control and venereal disease (VD) lectures.

Maggie Gilkes with the Canadian Women's Army Corps (the CWAC) remembers that the formal lectures were pretty dry and technical. The informal message was less so: "Remember girls, have an orange when you go to bed at night and another in the morning and nothing in between." She also remembers there was no swearing then, in spite of bombs bursting all around them in the worst days of the blitzkrieg. "The men wouldn't use four letter words in front of us," she recalled, "and women just didn't swear in those days." There was still that unmentionable code that women were somehow too fine to hear the rough language of men.

Other women serving overseas included 2,500 nurses and 38 doctors.

But most women kept the home fires burning—the title of a hugely popular song from World War I that made men and women on both sides of the ocean weep. The women did keep the home fires burning. That story has often been told. So has the story of the women who went into factories and did great jobs as welders and sheet metal workers. And so has the story of the women on the farm who learned to drive the tractors and bring in the crops. Amazing women, all of them, and many of them wearing pants—or trousers or slacks. Call the garments what you will, they had two legs, they were comfortable, they would not accommodate corsets or other harnesses (hallelujah!) and they were here to stay. The one good conse-quence of the war was that women claimed pants and never let them go.

Rationing was another job that fell to the women at home during the war. They had to figure out how to make meals for the family with reduced rations of sugar, butter, meat, coffee and tea. It was seri-ous business. You had a ration book with coupons in it, and the storekeeper sold you the rationed items only if you had the proper coupons. Many a wedding cake or birthday cake didn't get iced or even made. Many a garden was planted and tended to keep food on the table. Many an old hen got nervous when her egg production dropped.

Look at pictures of any group of women during that period. They're mostly slender. Little sugar, little butter and a more or less vegetarian diet kept them that way.

And as in World War I, there was knitting. Knitting connected the women to the men fighting overseas. Knit socks for them, knit constantly, knowing that what you held in your hands might warm and comfort a sol-dier, maybe your husband or your brother. At times women felt helpless to do anything real. Looking after the children and the home was real, but it was-n't war—and they yearned to do some-thing to show they were all in the war

During the war years, 1939–1945, many women took on nontraditional jobs. Some did so wearing their dresses, like these women shown sawing wood. (COURTESY RED DEER AND DISTRICT ARCHIVES)

Many women worked in factories and learned to love pants as did the female workers at this Edmonton factory. Others turned wrenches on locomotives.
(Courtesy Provincial Archives of Alberta)

together. So women knit. They knit while they got their hair cut, they knit during meetings and at church, they knit while teaching school, they knit while nursing the baby. Never have so many women known how to knit. Among women, the phrase, "I'm just ready to turn the heel" was perfectly understood as a major stage in the knitting of a sock—nothing to do with men who might be heels or bread that's down to the last crust. The socks found their way to the Red Cross and from there to the men overseas.

The worst hardship was knowing that as they thought about a son, husband or father, he might be dead in a bombed building, falling from a disabled airplane or drowning in a torpedoed ship. It didn't serve to have an imagination in the war years because there were so many ways to imagine death. One woman claimed she tried to send her son strength through her thought waves. "I'd just stand still and try so hard to affect him, to make him safe wherever he was." Her son did come home.

Mary Feschuk's son did not. Her story is told in *For King and Country*. She wrote so movingly about her loss that her words should conclude every story about the glory of war, every account by some hero, politician or spy that makes war into a glory game. When she heard that her nineteen-year-old son, George, had been killed in action, she said:

> My whole world fell apart. Relatives, neighbors and friends came to comfort us, but there was no comfort. The only comfort I had was from little Darlene who was only four. She would say, 'Mama, don't cry,' and try to wipe my tears but there was no stopping them—they were never wiped away. They fell in my garden, in the milk pail, in the bread dough.

Not big words about glory and conquest, but the words of a woman who mourned for her son as she continued the chores that fell to her. Bitter tears and bread dough—the realities of a woman's life in wartime.

Grace Budgeon in the Crossfield seniors' residence also talked about war and the constant threat around the world of more killing, more wars. "I feel betrayed," she said. "I worked hard, saved my money, hoping that I was making a better world for my grandchildren where they wouldn't want and wouldn't have to fight. But no, it's war again."

Abortion: The Word That Could Not Be Spoken

The subject of abortion looms over any discussion of the unmentionables in women's lives. It's difficult to discuss because such firmly held positions are entrenched on either side of a wide gulf. But abortion is part of women's history. It's the topic that has two extremes: it's either never mentioned at all; or, if a trial or a change in the law is concerned, it's constantly mentioned. There is no happy medium in this unhappy business, even into the twenty-first century.

The Supreme Court of Canada made abortions legal in 1988. Dr. Henry Morgentaler, who led the battle and still represents the cause, contends it's a quieter battle now. "The temperature has gone down," he says. "Most people today do not believe they should interfere in other people's lives. I think we've become much more tolerant."

Many of the early medical books warned women away from abortion entirely. It would result in "almost certain chronic invalidism for the remainder of a woman's life," warned the *Home Book of Modern Medicine* by Dr. J.H. Kellogg, a health guru of the early twentieth century. Not only that, but abortion led straight to "spiritual perdition," he warned. Kellogg's book was often found in western Canadian homes.

So abortion was a dirty little secret. It was illegal, and it was immoral by the standards of the day. But it existed and women knew it. If you'd been told by a doctor that you'd die if you had another baby, and you're pregnant because your husband thinks it's his right, what else do you think about? So you inquire carefully and a neighbor woman tells you to move rocks, really heavy rocks. That worked for her, she says. Another trusted friend suggests you fall down stairs, take scalding hot baths, drink some vile substance such as carbolic acid or turpentine mixed with sugar. Usually, nothing happened except that an overworked and distraught woman became even more stressed.

Some women heard through the grapevine that aboriginal women knew how to induce an abortion, so they sent away to the catalogue for a medication called the Indian Woman's Balm. The product did not, of course, promise anything but "relief for women's irregularities," a code for a substance likely to bring about an abortion. But most such products were simply a waste of money.

Sometimes women appealed to their doctors, and sometimes the doctors obliged with a surgical procedure that they'd hide under vague terms such as "vaginal cleansing" or "menopausal dysfunction" that could cover a host of problems. Doctors at least carried out the procedure under sterile conditions and kept an eye on their patients. If caught, they could get into trouble, although one Calgary doctor simply lost his license for a while and reportedly continued to offer the service to desperate women. A certain red brick house in the city is still known as the abortion house.

The last resort was the back-street butcher, often a woman who performed illegal abortions in her home. Desperate pregnant women found them by word of mouth and took their chances. Sometimes what the abortionist did worked, and sometimes it didn't. There are thousands of stories out there, but women who were forced into such desperate measures did not tell.

A doctor finally blew the whistle on one back-street practitioner, but it was only because one of the abortionist's customers died. In October 1935, Mrs. Susanna May Attridge of Moose Jaw, Saskatchewan, was charged with "intent to procure the miscarriage of Mrs. Eva Mazurkywicz, and did use or cause to be used on the person of the said Mrs.

Eva Mazurkywicz an instrument or other means, contrary to section 303 of the Criminal Code of Canada."

The case was confusing. At first Attridge was charged only with performing an abortion for Eva Mazurkywicz, who survived the abortion attempt and was therefore able to describe the whole grisly procedure. But the case of Catherine Kindrachuk was brought forth as evidence as well, and that opened up a whole new line of inquiry because Kindrachuk had died after an abortion performed by Attridge. Doctors who testified during the trial obviously wanted Attridge out of the abortion business. They had seen the sort of damage she could do and wanted a charge of manslaughter. The defense in turn kept reminding the court that Kindrachuk could have died from other things like septicemia, pneumothorax and streptococci, and besides the trial was all about Mazurkywicz.

The over two hundred pages of trial testimony tell of a sad and sordid business. Eva Mazurkywicz could barely speak English and had to have an interpreter in court. Attridge wanted twenty-five dollars for the abortion and eventually settled for ten dollars, a huge amount of money for a family in the 1930s. Eva bled and hurt and finally expelled what they called "products of conception" while alone at home. She then went to the nearest doctor who treated her. As for Kindrachuk, the story was that she had suffered for a very long time after her abortion until finally she died of poison throughout her body. The infection made her smell so bad that it was hard to give her proper nursing care. And even though the doctors knew there had been "some interference," they had to have better proof than just their own eyes and noses.

The grisly account at the trial at least made public the practices of back-street abortionists. Here's part of Eva Mazurkywicz's testimony, this time without an interpreter.

I come in the house and I knock the door and Mrs. Attridge open the door and then Mrs. Attridge said "come in" and I go in the office and she said "take a chair" and she said "what you got trouble" and I said "I not got very big trouble and I not know you can do something for me or not." And she said "what trouble" and I said "my blood stop and I have the last time" and she count on the fingers and she said that would be six weeks now . . . and she says "yes, I do for you." I says "how you do" and she says "oh, this not so much hard on you, I just open your [word is deleted from trial transcript] and I just put a tube inside.

So, Mrs. Attridge opened Eva's vagina with a vaginal speculum and inserted what looked to Eva like a nail or maybe a needle. Her testimony continues:

Put a little cotton around that and put it in a dish, like white water, and took that and put it in my private and she said "don't do that" [when Eva cried out in pain] and she took the other hand and push my stomach down and take that nail and make round and I yelled and says "hurt" and she says "hurt?" and I says "yes" and she says "you no want to pain nothing at all?"

And she took that needle and throw out that cotton batting and took another piece round and take the water and take again and push stomach back and it was just a little bad blood and throw out that too and throw another time and put it in the time and keep it stomach go down . . . and after she take some rubber tube and she put that in my private . . . and after she took

like another four pieces of cotton batting and put it to my private.

Attridge had disrupted the pregnancy with the needle or nail, and then inserted a soft rubber catheter through the cervix into the uterus. If everything went according to plan, the hollow tube of the catheter would carry away the bleeding she had caused and also the soft tissue of the developing fetus. Or it would irritate the uterus and thus cause spontaneous abortion. Either way, it would end the pregnancy. But it didn't happen for Eva immediately. She went home with the thing inside her "private" with the instructions to pull it out in four days. She did. Nothing happened. She went back to Attridge, who went through the whole gory process again. Still nothing happened. That's when Eva ended up so sick that she went to the local doctor and received treatment.

Attridge was found guilty of supplying an abortion to Eva Mazurkywicz, but not guilty in the abortion and death of Kindrachuk. She was sentenced to two years less one day to be served in the common jail for women in Battleford, Saskatchewan. The case was appealed in May 1936, but the records of the appeal and of her eventual release are buried in boxes in the prisoner registers in Battleford. What is known is that she did serve some time, but we don't know whether she went back to her old ways afterwards.

More Trouble with the Law

According to early North-West Mounted Police records for southern Alberta, mostly men ran afoul of the law. Women appear most often as victims. For example, according to the 1882 records for the Fort Macleod area, several men were accused of rape, two others were charged with having "carnal knowledge of a girl under the age of fourteen," one stole a stove and another was charged with "breaking into a dwelling house with intent to ravish." Other entries record instances of the more manly illegal arts: stealing horses, selling liquor to Indians, gambling, assault, larceny and highway robbery.

In those early records, women fall afoul of the law either for "concealing child birth" or for being "keeper or inmate of house of ill fame." The first concerns women who bore babies, tried to conceal the fact and caused the children to die or let them die. In one case recorded that year, the charge was deferred and there are no further details. The penalty for keeping or working in a brothel was a fine or fourteen to thirty days hard labor. Fines were always paid in preference to doing time. Other police reports from the early days show the same trend: men break the law in a variety of ways; women's misdemeanors involve sex.

The 1920 Calgary City Police report of crimes tried in police court during the previous year records 989 crimes committed by men. Most were for vagrancy, drunkenness and frequenting a bawdy house. Women were tried 135 times for vagrancy (a law used to arrest suspected prostitutes), drunkenness and being an inmate of a bawdy house. The female crime that didn't relate directly to sex was that of "insanity." Eighteen such charges were brought against women and twenty-five against men. There were also three charges against men for "seduction under promise of marriage," one for bigamy, one for rape and one for buying unwholesome eggs.

Buying unwholesome eggs seems a bit innocent compared to bigamy, for instance, but it was given the same importance on the list as the other charges.

Rape was not discussed in polite company. When Big Bear's men captured two women from the Frog Lake settlement during the North-West rebellion in 1885, newspapers had a field day speculating whether the two white women would have met a "fate worse than death." They never actually used the word *rape*, but the readers knew exactly what was at issue and waited anxiously for updates on the women's fate. For the record, they were not raped.

The public had more interesting and salacious reading during the 1933 trial of John Brownlee, premier of Alberta. A government secretary had charged him with seduction. Vivian MacMillan claimed he had taken her for rides in his car and had talked her into having sex with him because his wife was ill. She had frequently stayed over night at the Brownlee house, she testified, and had had sex with the premier in the bedroom he shared with his teenage son. The details were too delicious for newspapers to resist, and readers waited hungrily for the daily report of court proceedings and the lurid details of sexual encounters, the like of which they'd never read before.

Brownlee was found guilty of seduction and had to pay "damages" to both Vivian and her father. But there are those who now believe he was set up by Vivian's boyfriend who saw a way to make some money and who convinced her to go along with his plan. Brownlee

resigned as premier and went back to his life as a corporate lawyer in Calgary. Nobody seems to knows what became of Vivian or the boyfriend.

In days gone by, the word *seduce* meant to tempt or lure into sexual activity, and seduction was an illegal act, generally committed by a man upon a woman. As such, it had serious consequences involving jail for the generally male perpetrator and shame and disgrace for the fallen woman or soiled dove or poor butterfly. Mothers and fathers always had to be vigilant lest their daughters fall for the wiles of some sneaky seducer. If the seduction should lead to rape, another problem arose. Had the girl done everything she could to resist the attack? Bruises and torn clothing had to be shown, a previously chaste life had to be proven. Chastity was valued over life itself, or so it would seem from the purple prose that newspapers used to describe sexual assaults. In 1906 the Calgary *Morning Albertan* reported that a twenty-two-year-old woman in British Columbia had been murdered "defending her honor" and that the marks of violence upon her body denoted "the tragic tale of man's brutality and woman's brave resistance." The *Winnipeg Free Press* noted that the murdered woman "had died defending all that is dearest and best to womanhood—her honor." Better dead than raped apparently; better dead than suffer or utter the unmentionable word.

Nor would polite society mention the words *sex* or *intercourse.* According to the norms of the time, sexual relations were simply the burden women had to bear in order to have children. No need for talk. As Terry Chapman said,

It was generally assumed that the lust of the male was responsible for sexual encounters, and decent Christian women acted as passive or unwilling participants. A woman would participate in sex only if she was married, seduced, under the promise of marriage, or raped.

As for homosexuality, it was illegal until 1969 and was well hidden. Many people didn't even know there was such a thing. Ingeborg T. said, "I bet I was forty-five or fifty, and my husband too, before we even knew what a homosexual was. We were shocked, both of us." Again, mostly men in the early days were charged with commiting acts of homosexuality, with the occasional charge of buggery or sodomy appearing in early criminal records. Women seem to have stayed quiet and private about their sexual preferences. Who thought there was anything odd about two women living together years ago? They were just old maids sharing a house or young schoolteachers, bachelor girls together in the teacherage. If there was more to it than that, nobody said anything, including the women who were lesbian. Life went on peaceably, on the surface at least, until homosexuals began to come out and declare their sexual preference. Then the situation changed. Women schoolteachers who had lived together and eventually made their sexual orientation public were mocked, threatened with loss of jobs and shunned by their families. In 1967 Pierre Trudeau, then Minister of Justice, said famously, "There's no place for the state in the bedrooms of the nation." His Omnibus Bill, passed in 1969, removed criminal sanctions against same-sex practices between consenting adults. Lesbians could now live together openly with many of the same rights and obligations as heterosexual couples, but they could not marry. That's a more recent battle.

The lesson of history is that laws sometimes need to be changed. Until the 1920s, Albertans seemed to think it fair and right that women who became

Emily Murphy took her battles for women's rights to the Privy Council of England when she and four other Alberta women challenged the meaning of the word "persons" in the British North America Act. They won. Canadian women became "persons in law" in 1929.
(Courtesy Glenbow Archives)

pregnant out of wedlock should have to pay for it. After all, they had sinned. Virtue was a woman's responsibility, not a man's. But by the 1920s, some women's organizations had begun to question that thinking. Why should the woman bear total responsibility? She couldn't become pregnant without the man's contribution. So where was the man? The National Council of Women began to push for fairer laws for women, both for "good" women and for the "others." In 1923 the Alberta government brought in legislation requiring a man to support a child born out of wedlock if it could be proven he was the father. Before then, there was no such protection for women and children. But even after the bill was passed, women found it difficult to get legal support. Smart lawyers would get several men to admit to having had sex with the plaintiff so paternity could not be proven. One smart judge, hearing several men admit to having sexual relations with the woman in question, told them they could all contribute to the support of the child.

Emily Murphy, social activist, magistrate in a women's court in Edmonton and later a judge, was always concerned with women's legal rights. She came up with the idea of a "poor man's lawyer," lobbying for what eventually became

known as legal aid. She was speaking particularly on behalf of those who fell into prostitution. When charged with prostitution, the only way women could find the money for lawyer's fees was to continue working as prostitutes. It was a hopeless circle. It was almost as if the lawyers were also living on the avails of prostitution, Murphy said. Although it took some time, providing legal aid eventually became the norm.

Prostitution deserves its own place in the history of unmentionables because it is *not* unmentionable. You might think it would be. After all, it has to do with women and sex, a combination that was seldom mentioned by proper people years ago. But prostitution has been written about, has been the theme of plays and television shows, the subject of academic papers and is even included in war history. There's the story about Pearl Miller, the madam from Calgary the brave boys overseas remembered when one of them wrote on the wall of his barracks, "Never mind Pearl Harbor, remember Pearl Miller."

But prostitution is not a matter for jokes. What about the twelve-year-old prostitute whose words are quoted on the walls of the Calgary Police Museum: "What was I supposed to do? I was twelve years old, out on the streets in the freezing rain with nothing to eat and no place to stay."

What about Thelma Levy's story about her mother's friend who found herself pregnant out of wedlock? "I remember coming in after school and she and mother were both crying in the kitchen. She was leaving that night. Father didn't want her around me," Levy recalled. She left to go to the United States, where she had her baby and supported herself as a prostitute. When she came back to her hometown years later, she asked to see Thelma's little brother but "father wouldn't let her."

What about Rosalie, the aboriginal woman who was killed by one of her customers and then dismissed in the *Calgary Herald* report of the murder as "only a squaw. Her death does not matter much." At his trial for her murder, William (Jumbo) Fisk admitted that she had died by his hand. But she was only a squaw after all, he repeated, and in 1889 that opinion was commonly accepted. At 2:00 P.M. on the day of the trial, the jury retired to consider the testimony and reach a verdict. They deliberated for hours and couldn't agree. Judge Rouleau sent them back into the jury room after dinner and told the sheriff not to provide food, beds or lights until they came up with a decision. The next morning, they had arrived at a verdict: Fisk was not guilty.

Judge Rouleau would not accept the verdict and sent them back again. When they returned again to say they were deadlocked, Rouleau dismissed them and declared a new trial. Rumors flew through the town that one or more of the jurors had been bribed. That was never proven, but at the second trial Fisk was found guilty of manslaughter and sentenced to fourteen years. There were no women on that jury because women could not yet sit on juries.

Until the 1940s women were not allowed to join the police force either. Maggie Gilkes came home from serving in the CWAC in the Second World War and joined the Calgary police force in 1946. She was one of the first female members of a city police force in Canada. She was put on prostitute patrol, where eventually she got to know her "girls." If there was a complaint, Gilkes had the one-size-fits-all charge to use. She'd charge her girls with vagrancy and then take them to the Venereal Disease Clinic in downtown Calgary. Sometimes they went to jail until they had a clear smear—that is, until they tested negative for venereal disease. Other times, they had to promise to come regularly to the clinic for their shots. Because they liked the woman who ran the clinic, they generally kept their promises. But when jail time or treatment time was up, back they'd go to work on the streets. How they survived once they were too old for the game is never mentioned.

Guilty Until Proven Innocent

Aboriginal women had only to be aboriginal to be suspect of a crime. Unaccompanied women on the street were also immediately suspect. But other women could come under suspicion too. Judging one's neighbors and finding them wanting was very common. For instance, in 1917 the Calgary Children's Aid Society received an anonymous letter concerning a certain woman who seemed to have a great many male visitors while her husband was overseas. A caseworker was sent immediately to check up on Mrs. E. and her three children, aged four to eight. The house was tidy and comfortable, the report admitted, but when the caseworker warned Mrs. E. about the company she was keeping, Mrs. E. protested that the returned veterans who visited her home were friends of hers and her husband. "This is, of course, the usual excuse given," the authorities sniffed in their report.

Even though the authorities discov-

ered nothing that would warrant legal action, they decided that "the place will be reported to the detectives and if there are really suspicious circumstances as alleged in the anonymous note, a raid on the place will be made before long."

Another Calgary city report that year records the story of Mrs. K., also a soldier's wife:

> Mrs. K. has her two brothers-in-law, aged fourteen and sixteen with her, also a little adopted girl or niece, aged eleven years. The neighbors think she is receiving too much attention from a certain soldier, Sergeant S. Her husband is a prisoner of war.

A similar report states: "Called at _____ re[garding] a report of two soldiers' wives not living right. Mrs. L. has one child and Mrs. P. two. The house was untidy."

Although it would be nice to think that the soldiers' wives scolded the city inspectors who came round checking for men under the bed, it's not likely. The women knew the rules, and they knew the penalties.

In Edmonton, city fathers decided they needed a policy about the Mother's Allowance. This was money that today would be administered provincially as social assistance, but in the early years of the twentieth century was administered by the City of Edmonton. There were two sticky issues. Could mothers on allowance keep male boarders or lodgers? And should allowances be stopped where mothers are found guilty of immoral conduct?

The August 1923 recommendations of the city welfare committee included a report on Mrs. A, who had applied for relief:

Woman with two children of school age not eligible under Mother's Allowance Act. This woman who is a good tailoress but an indifferent housekeeper has been assisted considerably during the past two years. Committee consider that it is in the best interests of this woman who is not energetic and not happy under present conditions, that the children be placed in the Children's Aid Home this winter and the mother seek a position which will maintain herself and at least help maintain the children. Further assistance is to be refused this woman unless she accepts Welfare Board scheme.

The report on another Mrs. A. described a: "Widow with nine children under fourteen years of age. Incompetent and dirty housewife, untruthful and not generally reliable." The Committee recommended that "no pension be paid at the present time but that efforts be made by staff to raise standard of home."

Mrs. M. was treated more generously. "Deserted wife with four children," the report stated. "Committee recommends payment of rent in this case." Perhaps Mrs. M was simply a better housekeeper or perhaps she was seen as a "worthy" poor woman in contrast to the "unworthy" ones whom the Committee denied assistance.

Labels were routinely hung upon one another in earlier times. There was an unmentionably eager tendency to judge and criticize. An illegitimate baby? Get thee to a nunnery. Mental handicaps? Find an asylum and be silent about it. War? Put on your overalls. but take them off at the first possible moment. Underwear? Of course, even if it pinches and pokes.

In more recent years, however, the pendulum has swung the other way to the point that we have become almost anti-judgmental, especially in the matters discussed in this chapter. Mothers dare not criticize their daughter's bare belly buttons for fear they will harm youthful self-esteem, never mind the possibility of rape. Churches accept rather than reform. Adjectives have to be inclusive and neutral. Report cards affirm rather than reform. Rules are "preferred behaviors" and preferred behaviors are mere "guidelines for one's behavior"—that is, if one doesn't mind and the crick don't rise. And the world goes on turning and changing, making the unmentionable mentionable and the unspeakable speakable. And it has all happened so quickly. That's what seems paramount—the speed of all the changes.

Jane Jacobs, author and thinker, said in 2000: "Everything interesting happens at the edge of chaos." When it seems changes have been too extreme, too fast, it's chaos, that's all, and it's happened before. Don't mention it.

Chapter 6
We've Come Ungendered

★   ★   ★   ★   ★

THERE ARE THOSE WHO BLAME BIOLOGY for women's secondary place in the history of nations. Women have the babies, they point out, so women stay home instead of building nations and fighting wars—activities that seem to get a great deal more respect and ink than bearing and raising babies.

Could it be that underwear belongs somewhere on the continuum of blame? If a woman can't go to the bathroom because her corset is so tight she can't sit down, and her petticoats are so wide she can't go through a doorway, then she can't go far from home. And if she has to more or less disappear every time she menstruates because there's no convenient kit for handling it, it's no wonder she stays at home and reads, as Jane Austen's heroines do.

If a woman has to worry more about the state of her underclothes than the state of the nation, how can she run for parliament? In the 1950s if she was a nobody unless she's wearing "New Look" fashions by Christian Dior of Paris—dresses with soft, rounded shoulders, wasp waists and enormous spreading skirts designed for "flowerlike women"—how can she cram that vast skirt under a House of Commons desk? Indeed, how can she breathe, if she is cinched around the waist to achieve that tiny-waisted, full-bosomed shape?

If women were to get out there into the vigorous world of politics, economics, education and take an active part in that active world, they had to change their underwear.

Women's legs weren't seen at all in the early 1900s when members of the Red Deer Women's Institute posed on the church steps. By 1949, however, WI members from the Springvale area near Red Deer were allowing some leg to show. However, no pants on the scene yet even though they're cleaning the local school. (COURTESY RED DEER AND DISTRICT ARCHIVES)

Joanne Entwistle in *Body Dressing* agrees that underwear makes a difference to the life that is lived by the body.

Dress involves practical actions directed by the body upon the body which result in ways of being and ways of dressing, such as ways of walking to accommodate high heels, ways of breathing to accommodate a corset, ways of bending in a short skirt and so on.

If that's the case then it's fair to say that most of the underwear and much of the outerwear worn by European /American/Canadian women through the centuries—until the 1960s or thereabouts—limited the wearers. Women had to accommodate themselves to the underwear instead of the other way around. As fashion historian Ivan Sayers described it, it was beauty by impairment, beauty by inconvenience, beauty if it kills me.

The Women's Rescue Team at Number 2 coal mine in Canmore, Alberta, were apparently trained and ready to go underground to help with rescue efforts should they be needed. They were equipped with air filtering systems, flashlights, protective hats and shovels. They looked good; they looked ready. But the sad truth is that those young women never did get to go underground. Their long skirts, circa 1916, prevented any action. Who could climb ladders or wriggle through small underground spaces while wearing a petticoat and skirt?

Aboriginal women didn't lumber themselves with skirts and petticoats. Theirs was an active life, and they had to be able to move freely. They also had to be able to have their babies wherever the births happened and get on with life. European fur traders and explorers were often flabbergasted at the apparent ease with which the aboriginal women gave birth and returned to their regular duties. David Thompson wrote about an aboriginal woman in his exploring party who dropped behind the exploring party one afternoon and delivered a "little stranger." She caught up with them the next day, baby secure in his cradle board, and continued the journey. The European men weren't used to such exhibitions of female strength and didn't value it. It was somehow unseemly, unladylike. But what if European women had followed the example of Canada's First Nation women and became strong and capable, not cosseted by their clothing? Would we have experienced women's liberation earlier than we finally did? The role models were there, but no, the European influence was too strong and arrogant.

When the first generation of aboriginal women entered country marriages with white men in the fur trading posts, they produced daughters who knew both worlds. Some of the girls were sent out to schools and learned about corsets and modesty and other limiting factors, but they also knew their mothers. They too could have been the wave of the future for Canadian women, a mixture of aboriginal female strength and British tradition. But that wasn't allowed either. The bottom line was that they weren't white, they weren't European, they couldn't be real ladies. Only white women had that ability and if that status came with corsets that killed and rules that limited, women accepted their fate. Until, that is, until something snapped in the 1950s and 1960s. Maybe it was the last garter popping, but that snap changed the western world.

Think of the 1950s New Look—wasp waist, pointed breasts, full skirt—and try to imagine a female doctor wearing such a get-up in her office today or a female lawyer dressed like that in the courtroom. It wouldn't work. It says *woman* instead of *doctor* or *lawyer*. Not that the woman of today wants to deny her

gender, but she doesn't have to emphasize it all the time. The female lawyer likely wears a suit, formerly the uniform of men but now equally a woman's choice for business wear, because "it has come to represent neutrality and disembodiment," according to Entwistle. (Neutrality and disembodiment were the last things the New Look wearer wanted.) However, women are not yet quite as disembodied in our suits as men. We are still "located in the body," according to Entwistle, but at least the most sexualized zone—the breast area—is now covered by a suit jacket.

There is no such word as *ungender*. I'm surprised not to find it in our dictionaries since it fits the present state of gender relations. Certainly, the word is appropriate to underwear. Women wear sports bras that look like undershirts. They also wear undershirts. As for underpants, Queen Victoria would not be amused, but she might be surprised to find that, among the multitude of panty choices women have nowadays, open-crotch panties are back—but, of course, made from about 95 percent less cloth than was used for open-crotch knickers in 1850.

These days, petticoats have become costume. Garters have become a staple of love shops, and corsets, the dearly

The women's rescue team at Number Two mine in Canmore, Alberta, were ready and willing, but they never got to go underground. Skirts get in the way when you're trying to clamber down mine shafts. Oh, for a good pair of jeans. Though this picture hangs proudly in the Canmore Museum as a sign of early women's liberation, it's not that at all. It's just one more instance of clothing getting in the way of progress for women. (COURTESY CANMORE MUSEUM OF GEOSCIENCE ARCHIVES)

beloved of Queen Victoria and her descendants unto this day, have moved into the world of men.

Melanie Talkington, a young Vancouver woman has gone into the business of making corsets, the old-fashioned kind with whalebone and busks that push and pull the body into a shape the body doesn't really have. "Why ever would modern women want to wear one of these?" I asked. "We know better now."

"Oh, it's not women who are wearing them," she said. "It's men. The cross-dressers."

See why I think we need the word "ungender"?

The poet Anne Sexton, who died in 1974 at age forty-six, was thinking about gender in her poem "Consorting With Angels:"

I was tired of being a woman
Tired of the spoons and the pots
Tired of my mouth and my breasts
Tired of the cosmetics and silks . . .
I was tired of the gender of things.

There certainly are times in this brave new world when the gender of things gets complicated, even tiresome. Nellie McClung, Canadian author and activist, one of the Famous Five, put it more

simply: "I want to be a peaceful happy human, pursuing my unimpeded way through life, never having to explain, defend or apologize for my sex."

What would she have said about "The Good Wife's Guide"?

"The Good Wife's Guide" . . .

At the end of World War II, the lucky men came marching home again to rejoin their families or make new families—a good deal of family. The world was good again. Women took off their overalls and left the factories, farms and offices. Or at least most of them did. Some had discovered that they liked working outside the home, but they kept quiet about it. It wasn't time yet to challenge the notion that men's work and women's work were different and separate. It was all right for widows or "old maids" to work, but married women were expected to stay home and be housewives. It was an honorable calling, and most women accepted it happily.

Women's underwear went ultra-feminine in the first few years after the war. It was really rather fun to be a woman again, to be able to dress up and dance perhaps without the horrid fearful thought of war always on your mind. Or to get out of your overalls and say to your husband who had miraculously survived, "It's your turn, here's the milk pail." The world had for so long been under the awful shadow of bad news that to have it over was such a relief. Bring on the frills and ruffles and waist-cinching styles. Time to party. So back into the fashion world came tight girdles, pointy spiral-stitched bras, waist cinchers, nylons, garters and slips. That's when the slip, the elusive undergarment that must never show, became a fluffy, scratchy, crinoline petticoat that was supposed to show (occasionally and tastefully) under the full skirts of the New Look fashions or the later poodle skirt. For a while women were almost back to the hooped petticoats of the 1800s. A crinoline petticoat made sitting difficult. To launder the thing, it had to be stiffened with starch and ironed to within an inch of its life. Why did women wear these things? Because everyone else was wearing them and they could.

In the world of marriage, things went a bit overboard as well. "The Good Wife's Guide" in the May 1955 edition of *Housekeeping Monthly* advised women.

1. Have dinner ready. Plan ahead, even the night before, to have a delicious meal ready on time for his return. This is a way of letting him know you have been thinking of him and are concerned about his needs. Most men are hungry when they come home and the prospect of a good meal (especially his favorite dish) is part of the warm welcome needed.

2. Be a little gay and a little more interesting for him. His boring day may need a lift and one of your duties is to provide it.

3. Over the cooler months of the year, you should prepare and light a fire for him to unwind by. Your husband will feel he has reached a haven of rest and order, and it will give you a lift too. After all, catering for his comfort will provide you with immense personal satisfaction.

4. Prepare the children. Take a few minutes to wash the children's hands and faces (if they are small), comb their hair and, if necessary, change their clothes. They are little treasures and he would like to see them playing the part. Minimize all noise. At the time of his arrival, eliminate all noise of the washer, dryer, or vacuum. Try to encour-

The secret is freedom and that means no bras or girdles. You got to do what you want to do and wear what you want to wear. Everybody is so hung up on the matching game — the shoes have to match the bag which matches the coat and dress. But the big question is, is it matching your soul?
— Janis Joplin in the Village Voice, quoted in The Lace Ghetto.

age the children to be quiet.

5. Listen to him. You may have a dozen important things to tell him, but the moment of his arrival is not the time. Let him talk first—remember, his topics of conversation are more important than yours.

6. Make the evening his. Never complain if he comes home late or goes out to dinner or other places of entertainment without you. Instead, try to understand his world of strain and pressure and his very real need to be at home and relax.

7. Don't greet him with complaints and problems.

8. Don't complain if he's late home for dinner or even if he stays out all night. Count this as minor compared to what he might have gone through that day.

9. Don't ask him questions about his actions or question his judgment or integrity. Remember, he is the master of the house and as such will always exercise his will and truthfulness. You have no right to question him.

10. A good wife always knows her place.

Of course, there were lots of women who didn't read *Housekeeping Monthly* and wouldn't put up with such nonsense. Still, the codes of gendered behavior prevailed. Women fulfilled themselves through their husbands and the success of their children. Men were self-made. Women made supper. Men made money and decisions. Women sometimes worked outside the home, but they made less money than a man doing the same work. Men made that decision. And so on. It was a revolution asking to happen, and it did. It was known as the women's movement.

... Followed, of Course, by the Women's Movement

The women's movement in the 1960s challenged almost everything, especially the sort of patronizing attitude toward women revealed in the "Good Wife's Guide." Some wives may have followed the recommendations, but there were others who wanted more out of life than a pat on the head. Enter consciousness raising, Canada's Royal Commission on the Status of Women in 1967, Gloria Steinem and *Ms.* magazine, Betty Friedan and *The Feminine Mystique*, angry editorials and placard-waving protests, legal challenges, anger at the dinner table. Even underwear joined the fray when women burned their bras. It's such a perfect symbolic gesture. Although a number of writers and researchers have tried to track down an actual bra-burning event complete with pictures, no one has been able to find any. Perhaps it was more a case of "I Dreamed I Burned My Maidenform Bra."

All the same, the very idea is indicative of the enormous changes in women's lives brought on by the social revolution, the women's movement. One of the first fights in the revolution involved the birth control pill. Women were finally able to say the words *birth control*. They sang them, chanted them, put them on placards, wrote newspaper articles about them, talked about the issue and analyzed it. Older women watched from the sidelines because they weren't used to mentioning such personal issues. Younger women marched. It was a grand fight, and it changed the world.

With the pill, women were able to control when and if they'd have babies. Never before had they been able to control reproduction while still having sex whenever they chose. It was the have-sex-whenever part that upset opponents of the pill the most. Women, they said, would turn into trollops and sluts, hav-ing sex willy-nilly, here and there, maybe even in the streets. And some of that has come true. Women do have sex with Willy and Nilly too, if she's around, and sometimes it's on the streets. On the television or movie screen we witness simulated sex, clothes that scream sex, songs with words so explicit they make a grandmother blush, sex with everything. It's so common-place that it's become almost boring except to those who find it shocking.

All because of one little white pill.

Gloria Steinem, in *Outrageous Acts and Everyday Rebellions,* says the pill has elevat-ed reproductive rights to a universal human right at least as basic as freedom of speech or assembly. A woman has the right to decide the use of her body. What an amazing change in minds and hearts and governments that reflects! It's a revolution, a giant step, a freedom that could not have been imagined in Queen Victoria's time or even at the tentative beginning of the women's movement.

As if the pill weren't a big enough fight in the 1960s, women added to that battle almost every real or perceived wrong done to them for centuries and turned it into a fight not just for birth control but for equal rights in all human endeavor. We wanted the right

The young woman doing her homework is wearing the blue jeans that made headlines in Calgary, Alberta, in 1957. She was expelled from school for wearing them, but, with the help of the local newspa-per and a growing awareness of human rights, she was soon back in the classroom. (COURTESY GLENBOW ARCHIVES, NA-5600-8236A)

Ginger Laughlin wore her blue jeans to school in the early 1950s in Grande Prairie, and not a word was said except, "Where can I buy some just like that?" (COURTESY GINGER KELLY)

to work outside the home, we wanted our work to be valued in the same way as men's, we wanted day care and better divorce laws, we wanted shelters for battered women and education for battering men, we wanted to run for city council and be taken seriously, we wanted equal opportunities at colleges and universities. It was an absolutely necessary social revolution.

Another change that came about in those heady days of protest was pants—pants for one and pants for all. As women loosened their minds about womanhood, they began loosening up their clothes as well. Without girdles, garters and nylons, without slips that had to be discreet and under control, without all those clothes that cosseted and restricted, women were new people. Some women went so far as to wear jeans, though there was a considerable fuss about that at first. In 1957 a schoolgirl in Calgary wore jeans to class. She was promptly expelled and told to stay away until she could dress decently. She hadn't sassed the teachers or used bad words—she had simply worn a pair of fairly baggy jeans to school. The story made headlines in the local paper, but it was a losing battle. Soon all the girls were wearing jeans to school or slacks to the office or trousers to church or pants wherever.

In the early 1970s, at age sixty, my mother bought her first pantsuit and we never saw her legs again. She wasn't showing solidarity for the women's movement—"that women's lib bunch," as she put it—but she was sold on pants. I told her once that she should be careful because a change in clothing signaled a change in thought and she might starting writing slogans like "Women United For Change" on the side of our barn. She rolled her eyes and told me in no uncertain terms that her preference for pants had nothing to do with the women's movement. But it did. She didn't have to wear an ugly, unyielding corset anymore, and she didn't have to worry about garters and nylons and shoes that hurt. She could dress comfortably in this brave new world of fashion,—thanks to the dreaded women's lib bunch.

Pants should possibly be right up there with Germaine Greer and Betty Friedan as pivotal to the women's movement. The women who stayed behind while their men fought the war overseas got used to wearing overalls or coveralls in the fields or the factories. Suddenly, their bodies were capable, and they felt good. True, they took those liberating pants off for a while during the silly post-war years. But the muscle memory

Women weren't just wearing jeans, they were making them. Out of the kitchen into the factory—that was the story of the 1960s. This is a group of female workers in the GWG factory in Edmonton.

(Courtesy Provincial Archives of Alberta)

The women in the advertisement are flying, but it was tough to walk, let alone fly, when wearing a long-line corset or panty girdle. It was when the corset and girdle came off that flying was accomplished, at least metaphorically.

(COURTESY *CHATELAINE* MAGAZINE)

was still there, the memory of a freedom not possible in crinolines and long-line bras.

Maybe that's why the women's movement felt so right when it came along. It brought back pants and the freedom they represent. If you take off corsets in order to wear pants, you can breathe. Unhitch the garters and you can walk. Throw away the layers of petticoats and you can get through doors. Get rid of your inflatable bra and you can breathe deeply. Pull on your pants and take on the world. That's what the men and women who fought the first battles of the women's liberation movement did—they took on the world and changed it. The revolution still simmers, of course. Stories of individual battles continue, but there's more time for reflection now. It can never be said that the battle has been won, that the soldier can lay down her arms, but many battles *have* been won and they are now being analyzed and written about in scholarly books and articles. Women's private lives are not unmentionable anymore. But the story of the other unmentionables—the stories in this book—have not been told before. They are the stories of the harnesses that worked on our minds as well as our bodies, all the silences that surrounded us and that silenced us in turn. Our unmentionable history.

Sources and Suggested Reading

Allison, Dorothea. Letters 1913-1922. Royal B.C. Museum. "Living Landscapes." http://www.livinglandscapes.bc.ca/thomp-ok/allison/index.html

Barker, George. *Forty Years a Chief*. Winnipeg: Peguis, 1979.

Barr, Estelle. *Folklore*. Saskatchewan History and Folklore Society, (Winter 1985-86).

Battye, Brenda. Personal memoir. Vancouver.

Beck, Janice Sanford. *No Ordinary Woman: The Biography of Mary Schäffer Warren*. Calgary: Rocky Mountain Books, 2001.

Bird, Madeline. With the assistance of Sister Agnes Sutherland. *Living Kindness: The Dream of My Life: The Memoirs of Metis elder, Madeline Bird*. Yellowknife NWT: Outcrop, 1991.

Blatz, Dorothy. "Keeping Warm." *Folklore*. Saskatchewan History and Folklore Society, (Spring 1994).

Brick's Hill, *Berwyn and Beyond*. Berwyn: Berwyn Centennial Committee, 1968. http://www.ourroots.ca/e/toc.asp?id=3634

Carstairs, Sharon and Tim Higgins. *Dancing Backwards: A Social History of Canadian Women in Politics*. Winnipeg: Heartland Associates, 2004.

Colley, Kate Brighty. *While Rivers Flow: Stories of Early Alberta*. Saskatoon: Prairie Books, 1970.

Cunnington, C. Willett, and Phillis Cunnington. *The History of Underclothes*. New York: Dover Publications, 1992.

Entwistle, Joanne and Elizabeth Wilson, eds. *Body Dressing*. New York: Berg, 2001.

Ewanchuk, Michael. *Reflections and Reminiscences, Ukrainians in Canada*. Winnipeg: M. Ewanchuk, 1994.

Fahlman, Jean. "Washday Blues." *Folklore*. Saskatchewan History and Folklore Society, (Autumn 1999).

Flannery, Regina. *Ellen Smallboy: Glimpses of a Cree Woman's Life*. Rupert's Land Record Society series; Montreal: McGill-Queen's University Press, 1995.

Fontanel, Beatrice Support and Seduction: The History of Corsets and Bras. New York: Harry N. Abrams, 2001.

Fortier, Alice (Bennett) et al. *Adoptees are Angels*.

Granatstein, J.L. and Norman Hillmer, comp. *First Drafts: Eyewitness Accounts from Canada's Past*. Toronto: Thomas Allen, 2002.

Hibbert, Christopher, ed. *Queen Victoria in her Letters and Journals*. London: John Murray Publishers, 1984.

Hopkins, Monica. *Letters From a Lady Rancher*. Intro by Sheilagh S. Jameson. Calgary: Glenbow Museum Publication, 1981.

Hungry Wolf, Beverly. *Daughters of the Buffalo Women: Maintaining the Tribal Faith*. Skookumchuck, B.C. : Canadian Caboose Press, 1996.

Hungry Wolf, Beverly. *The Ways of My Grandmothers*. New York: William Morrow, 1980.

Jackson, Mary Percy. *Suitable for the Wilds: Letters from Northern Alberta, 1929-1931*. Ed. Janice Dickin McGinnis. Toronto: University of Toronto Press, 1995.

Jefferis, B.G. and J.L. Nichols. *Search Lights on Health, Light on Dark Corners: A Complete Sexual Science and a Guide to Purity and Physical Manhood, Advice to Maiden, Wife and Mother, Love, Courtship and Marriage*. Toronto : J.L. Nichols, 1894.

Kellogg, J.H. *The Home Book of Modern Medicine*. Battle Creek, MI: Good Health Publishing Co., 1914.

Keswick, J.B. *Woman, Her Physical Culture & Including Her Dress, Habits, Womanhood and Her Diseases and How to Cure Them*. N.p: n.d.

Land of Hope and Dreams. Grimshaw AB: Grimshaw and District Historical Society, 1980.

Langford, Nanci "Modesty and Meaning in Alberta Local Histories." *Aspenland II, On Women's lives and Work in Central Alberta*. Ed. David Ridley. Red Deer: Central Alberta Regional Museums Network and Central Alberta Historical Society, 2003. http://www.albertasource.ca/aspenland/eng/society/article_meaning_modesty.html

MacEwan, Garnt. *Fifty Mighty Men*. Saskatoon: Western Producer Prairie Books, 1975.

Mackie, Marlene. *Gender Relations in Canada: Further Explorations.* Toronto: Butterworths, 1991.

Maguire, Constance A. "Kate Simpson Hayes, Agnes Agatha Hammell, and 'the slur of illegitimacy'." *Saskatchewan History.* Fall1998 50.2.

Manchester, William. *The Last Lion: Winston Spencer Churchill.* Toronto: Little, Brown, 1983.

McClung, Nellie. *In Times Like These.* 1915. Toronto: University of Toronto Press, 1972.

McDonald, Pat. *Where the River Brought Them: 200 Years at Rocky Mountain House & Area.* Rocky Mountain House AB: Town of Rocky Mountain House Bicentennial History Book Committee, 2000.

McNeil, Eileen M. "Women of vision and compassion: the foundation of health care in Calgary." *Alberta History* (Winter 2002) 50.1.

Melendy, Mary Ries. *The Science of Eugenics.* Harrisburg PA: Minter, 1904.

Melendy, Mary Ries. *Vivilore, The Pathway to Mental and Physical Perfection: The Twentieth Century Book for Every Woman.* Toronto: J.L. Nichols Co., 1904.

Mosquitoes, Muskeg and Memories: A History of Wesley Creek and Three Creeks. McKinney Hall History Book Committee, 1985.

Norris, Marjorie Barron. *Sister Heroines: The Roseate Glow of Wartime Nursing, 1914-1918.* Calgary: Bunker to Bunker Publishing, 2002.

Nunes, Maxine and Deanna White. *The Lace Ghetto.* Toronto: The New Press, 1972.

Palmer, Alexandra, ed. *Fashion: A Canadian Perspective.* University of Toronto Press, 2004.

Potrebenko, Helen. *No Streets of Gold: A Social History of Ukrainians in Alberta.* Vancouver: New Star Books, 1977.

Savage, Candace. *Cowgirls.* Toronto: Greystone Books, 1996.

Schultz, Judy. *Mamie's Children: Three Generations of Prairie Women.* Red Deer: Red Deer College Press, 1997.

Shadows of the Neutrals. Coronation AB: Old-Timer's Centennial Book Committee, 1967.

Silverman, Elaane Leslau. *The Last Best West : Women on the Alberta Frontier, 1880-1930.* Montreal: Eden Press, 1984.

Steinem, Gloria. *Outrageous Acts and Everyday Rebellions.* New York: Holt, 1983.

Strong-Boag, Veronica. "Growing Up Female." *Readings in Canadian History.* Ed. R. Douglas Francis and Donald Smith. 3rd. Toronto: Holt, 1990.

Sweaty Brows & Breaking Plows: History of Mayton-May City Districts. May City-Mayton Historical Society, 1991.
The Roaring Twenties. The Best of Times: A History of High River & District 3. High River: Century Books, 2002.

The Spirit of Ghost Pine. Ghost Pine AB: The Ghost Pine Community Group, History Book Committee, 1990.

Thompson, Shirley Keyes. *A Prairie Wife's Tale.*

Tingley, Ken, ed. *For King and Country.* Edmonton: Alberta Provincial Museum and Reidmore Books, 1995.

Trails to Little Corner. Namaka AB: Namaka Community Historical Committee, 1983.

Tuck, Esme. *In Peace River Chronicles: Eighty-One Eye-Witness Accounts from the First Exploration in 1793 of the Peace River Region of British Columbia, Including the Finlay and the Parsnip River Basins.* Ed. Gordon Emerson Bowes. Vancouver: Prescott, 1963.

Van Kirk, Sylvia. " 'The Reputation of a Lady': Sarah Ballenden and the Foss-Pelly Scandal." *Manitoba History* 11, 1986.

Van Kirk, Sylvia. *Many Tender Ties: Women in Fur-Trade Society, 1670-1870.* Winnipeg: Watson & Dwyer, 1980.

Wagon Trails Plowed Under: A History of Eagle Valley, Sundre East, and Sangro. Eagle Valley AB: Eagle Valley Book Club, 1977.

Yeomans, Amelia. *Dr. Amelia Yeomans.*[Winnipeg]: Manitoba, Historic Resources Branch, 1985. Qtd. in "Dr. Amelia Yeomans (1842-1913)." U of Man. Health Sciences Library. http://www.umanitoba.ca/libraries/units/health/resources/womhist/ayeomans.html

Nancy Millar has been a columnist for the Calgary Herald, a television producer and newsreader for CBC Calgary and is the author of six books including *Remember Me As You Pass By, Once Upon A Tomb, The Famous Five* and *The Final Word.* She is a frequent speaker on historical subjects for teachers' conventions, women's organizations, community and church groups, genealogical societies and, of course, historical societies. Somewhat surprised to be on the cutting edge of outhouse culture, she judged an outhouse race in Cochrane, Alberta, some years ago and since then has received numerous stories about outhouses. Coming soon—a book on outhouses? She is a wife, mother and grandmother and lives in Calgary.